ILLUSTRATED TALES OF
KENT

NAOMI DICKINS

AMBERLEY

This book is dedicated to my own Kent ancestors and to Kentish folk and the folk of Kent, past, present, and future.

First published 2023

Amberley Publishing
The Hill, Stroud
Gloucestershire, GL5 4EP

www.amberley-books.com

British Library Cataloguing in Publication Data.
A catalogue record for this book is available from the British Library.

ISBN 978 1 3981 0183 8 (paperback)
ISBN 978 1 3981 0184 5 (ebook)

Origination by Amberley Publishing.
Printed in Great Britain.

Contents

Introduction

Of the countless tales and legends entwined with the long, rich history of Kent, this little collection hardly represents a fraction, but, in it, you will find stories associated with the comings and goings of the myriad 'incomers' and 'invaders' who have chosen to make Kent their home, as well as folk tales of local customs that speak of a long, deep, and colourful rural heritage. Heroes and villains jostle for our attention, whilst rebels and royals fight for our loyalty, and ghosts threaten to haunt the darkest corners of the night long after we finish reading. Even the ancient landscape calls out for us to listen to its ageless narrative. Kent is a county that has many stories to tell; these are tales and legends that have evolved gradually and for which there are, often, no definitive sources. I have selected a few and have done my best to present them here with as much historical accuracy as possible – for example, in consulting parish registers, eyewitness accounts, and newspaper reports where they exist. For the rest, I hope you will forgive the artistic licence and enjoy the stories that follow. Now, if you are sitting comfortably, let us begin.

I

Kentish Men or Men of Kent?

The silver stripe of the River Medway divides the county of Kent into two unequal parts; even the county town is bisected by it, having grown up on both banks. Tradition has it that Men and Maids of Kent hail from the north and east of the county, while Kentish Men and Maids come from the south and west. According to Bede, the distinction stems from the Anglo-Saxon settlement of the area in the fifth century; he tells us how north-eastern Kent was settled by Jutes, but the remainder of the county by Saxons, and modern archaeological evidence appears to supports his narrative.

Six hundred years later, it seems that territorial distinctions were still clearly delineated, and the two parties viewed the Norman invasion from very different

Paul Sandby, *A Distant View of Maidstone, from Lower Bell Inn, Boxley Hill,* 1802.

perspectives. The Jutish Men of Kent challenged the incomers and salvaged their independence, preserving their tradition of gavelkind (or 'give all kind' – the ancient system of partible inheritance) along with elements of their laws and customs. The Saxon Kentish Men – perhaps due to a closer cross-Channel relationship – enabled the Conqueror's half-brother, Bishop Odo of Bayeaux, to transform Kent into a politically significant and prosperous Norman stronghold.

So much ancient history? Perhaps, but there were separate east and west Kent cricket teams until the formation of the Kent County Cricket Club in 1842 and, even as recently as the 1960s, the county retained two separate army regiments: the East Kent Buffs and the Queen's Own Royal West Kent Regiment. Travelling from one side of the county to the other, the differences are distinct and there is a feeling that, although the two halves stand very closely together, they might also stand back-to-back …

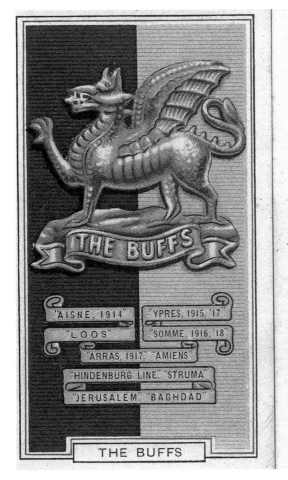
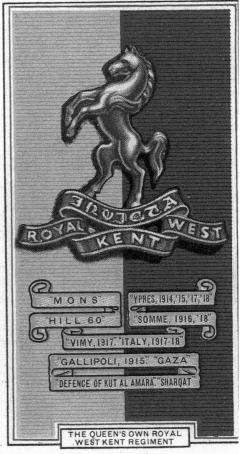

Insignia of the two Kent regiments.

2

Hengist and Horsa

Influential but enigmatic, the Anglo-Saxons were the founders of medieval English society. In Kent, their legacy is a foundation myth of heroism, love, treachery and betrayal, and it was washed in with a small band of longships that docked in a port on the north Kent coast.

Fifth-century England was a place of change and, for some, opportunity. Under Roman occupation, England flourished as a place of vibrant cultural exchange, benefitting from the cosmopolitan make-up of its occupying army and the eclectic diaspora of continental settlers. As the Empire's control wavered, pockets of robust and sustainable agricultural communities began to emerge, but the departure of the imperial military machine also left England vulnerable to raiders and the spectre of war. Whether tempted by the prospect of land and independence, or enticed by tales of magic and gold, many ventured across the North Sea towards the mist-shrouded island of Albion in search of new beginnings. Of course, not all those who came were peaceable and there were instances of significant conflict between incomers and the increasingly challenged inhabitants. St Gildas described the savage brutality of the Picts and Scots – 'cruel enemies' of the Britons – that descended the moment the Romans 'left the island never to return'.[1] His account echoes with his countrymen's plaintive calls upon the Roman administration for aid. In the mid-440s, they wrote: 'The barbarians drive us to the sea ...the sea throws us back on the barbarians: thus, two modes of death await us, we are either slain or drowned.'[2] Time and again, their pleas went unheard until the Britons' king, Vortigern, making 'the same request to the princes of the Angles', secured an alternative alliance.[3]

This collectors' tea card presents a romanticised picture of the arrival of Hengist and Horsa in Kent.

On the northern shores of modern-day Germany, a group of young men were preparing for a sea voyage. According to the long-held traditions of their people, they were bidding farewell to families, friends, and the lives they had known, striking out into new territories. Their leaders, Hengist and Horsa, noble sons of Wihtgils, were descended from Woden, wise All-Father of the Old Saxons. Their journey would take them westwards, across the Northern Sea, and into Kent, down the Wantsum Channel. Arriving at Ebbsfleet, these 'tall strangers' who 'excelled all the rest both in nobility and gracefulness of person' were invited to the king's court at Canterbury. Hengist wasted no time in offering the king the service of their 'three brigandines … full of armed men' in return for a place to settle and – convinced that they had been sent by God to bring relief to his long-assailed people – Vortigern joyfully agreed. The Pictish onslaught was soon renewed, but the Celtic raiders were no match for these German warriors, whose triumph was swift and decisive. Buoyed by victory, the brothers asked the king's permission to send for reinforcements; 'invite over whom you please,' gushed Vortigern, revelling in the glory of long-awaited triumph, 'you shall have no refusal from me in whatever you desire,' so they sent word for their brethren and 'men came from three nations of Germany: from the Old Saxons, the Angles, and the Jutes.'[4]

The descendants of these incomers would settle and prosper in the British Isles. They were the grandsires of the warriors of Hastings, but in the 400s, the Saxons had yet to win their kingdom. Outsiders, immigrants, and perhaps worst of all pagan, they were regarded with distrust, 'a race hateful to both God and men,' according to Gildas, who paints Hengist's company as the 'wolves in … the sheep-fold'[5]; although they came 'at first to help the Britons,' he wrote, 'later they fought against them.'[6]

The arrival of Hengist and Horsa, from Richard Verstegan's 1605 *Restitution of Decayed Antiquities*.

Uninterrupted success made the Saxons bold and gave Hengist confidence to make repeated demands of the king; Vortigern, trying to juggle the interests of his own nobles with appeasing his new champions was unable – or unwilling – to satisfy the Saxon's ambition. However, the determined Hengist played a winning hand in sending for his daughter, Rowena. Vortigern – to the dismay of his Christian council – became 'inflamed with her beauty' and, so they alleged, was bewitched into falling in love with the pagan foreigner. Thoroughly besotted, in return for her hand, Vortigern offered Hengist the Kingdom of Kent – without first consulting his nobles, its governor, or his own sons. This rash action, fuelled by the king's overwhelming, private passion, would sow the seeds of war.

From the very outset, Hengist had been mustering an army: followers landed every month and his sons' arrival was accompanied by 'three hundred ships filled with soldiers'. Dismayed at his father's blindness to Hengist's machinations, Vortimer, the king's eldest son, emerged as the figurehead for resistance to Saxon domination. Rallying a redoubtable force of disillusioned Britons, Vortimer mounted a sustained attack on the Saxon incomers, defeating them and driving them back three times, before engaging them at Aylesford, where both he and Hengest would lose a brother in the fray. The Saxons retreated to Thanet, where Vortimer's determined forces harried them into submission. Their triumph would be short-lived; Vortimer died soon after, and Hengist seized the opportunity to treat with Vortigern. A meeting was arranged and Vortigern, ever trusting, had no inkling that his father-in-law had devised a treacherous plan. Hengist arrived with few attendants, but an army followed in his wake and every man of his party came armed with the knife or seax from which these legendary warriors had earned their name. At Hengist's command, 460 of the king's loyal men fell to the Saxon blades. Vortigern was spared – but for the price of his kingdom.

Canterbury chronicler Thomas Sprott tells us that Hengist's rule in Kent began 'in the eighth year of the arrival of the Anglii in Britain, which Nennius tells us was in 447, and he reigned for twenty-four years'[7], after which, he was succeeded

AYLESFORD.

Aylesford. The Anglo-Saxon Chronicle tells us that Horsa was killed in battle here in 455.

by Aesc, his son, who secured a final, decisive victory over the remaining Britons at Crayford. Within a century, his dynasty would bring forth Aethehlbert, Kent's first Christian king, and, when William of Normandy looked to claim his inheritance, it was not the Roman Britannia that he sought to rule but Engla-land, the kingdom of the Anglo-Saxons.

Of course, there is much academic debate about the existence of Hengist and Horsa; many perceive them as merely mythological figures, conjured to furnish the story of the Britons' fall to the Saxons. The name 'Hengist' appears in early Scandinavian-origin literature, but there is no way of proving that the disparate references pertain to the same individual, let alone whether that individual was real or fictional. On the other hand, there is a persistent argument for the brothers' historical authenticity, and each is commemorated as 'Conqueror of Britain' in King Ludwig I's Regensburg Walhalla.[8] None of our ancient forebears are any more 'real' to us than the parchments which bear their names down the centuries and Hengist and Horsa have certainly weathered those centuries well enough to deserve their place in our county's heritage.

At Pegwell Bay, there is a replica of an eighth-century Viking longship, the *Hugin*, a reconstructed vessel that sailed from Denmark to Thanet in 1949 in commemoration of Hengist's and Horsa's arrival.

(© Helmut Zozmann CC BY-SA 2.0)

3
Holly Boys and Ivy Girls

The *Gentleman Magazine* for February 1779⁹ contains an enquiry about 'an odd kind of sport' discovered by the correspondent in 'a little obscure village' whilst travelling through Kent. The writer says they came upon a group of girls gathered around the burning effigy of 'Holly Boy', which the girls said they had stolen from the village boys. Elsewhere in the village, those boys were similarly engaged in burning 'Ivy Girl', another 'crude effigy' which they had stolen from their female counterparts. Both groups were making 'loud huzzas, noise, and acclamations' but, when the writer questioned the village's more mature residents as to the origin of the custom, they could only ascertain that 'it had always been a sport' there, at Shrovetide.

In the 1700s, on May Day morning, the boys of Frindsbury and the boys of Rochester used to meet on Rochester Bridge to re-enact an incident in their shared, medieval history. A procession of the brethren of Rochester Priory, finding themselves caught in a sudden storm, became anxious for their safety as the strong breeze picked up around them. With their lights guttering and their banners flailing in the wind, the monks sought permission to pass through the orchard of the Strood Hospital and were granted passage by the Master of the House. However, he did not take the time to consult with the hospital brethren in this decision so, when the Rochester monks were espied between the apple trees, they were immediately taken for trespassers. A band of Frindsbury men was rapidly assembled, each armed with a bat or club, to beat the monks and frighten them away from the property. Rather than face the Frindsbury men's aggression, the monks turned tail and headed back out into the rising gale. When news of this incident reached the cathedral prior, a robust and immediate demonstration of penance was demanded of the Frindsbury men; they were commanded to process to the cathedral on Whit Monday, carrying the weapons with which they had committed the heinous offence, and there beg forgiveness of their sins. This spectacle was to occur every year until the death of the last of the men involved and was commemorated thereafter by boys and young men in a rowdy, annual skirmish."

4

The White Horse of Kent

The majestic white horse of Kent is instantly recognisable, but the history of the strong association of the silver stallion with this region has long faded into legend. The emblem might represent the valiant steed of the Saxon Horsa; there are examples of the symbol in Stuart histories of the period, such as Richard Verstagen's 1605 depiction of 'the arrival of the first ancestors of English-men out of Germanie', and John Speed's 1611 portrait of Hengist in his *Saxon Heptarchy*, but the achievement was only granted to the county by the Royal College of Arms as recently as 1933.

Artist Charles Newington designed a striking hill carving of Kent's white horse as a Millennium landmark. Inspired by the prehistoric Uffington Horse in Oxfordshire and set into the Downs above the Eurotunnel Shuttle terminus at Cheriton, the Folkestone White Horse bids welcome and farewell to around 10 million cross-Channel travellers every year. Construction of the 90 metres artwork took place in the early summer of 2003, undertaken by a team of Gurkhas (stationed at nearby Shornecliffe Barracks), who were directed by Newington via a radio link.

Above: Hengist, displaying the emblem of the white horse, from the Kent map page in John Speed's 1611 *Saxon Heptarchy*.

Right: The White Horse.

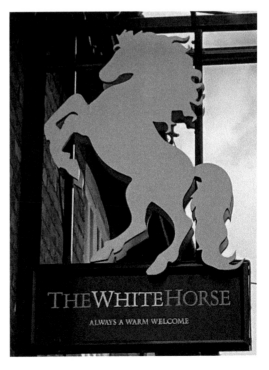

5
Penenden Heath Witch Trial, 1652

Stand on Penenden Heath recreation ground on a late summer's evening and you'll likely see a few joggers, the odd dog-walker and perhaps a handful of loping teenagers kicking a ball about. In the dappled shade of the lime and oak leaves, it is a fair enough prospect, with a view that stretches away towards the Downs. There is a plaque to commemorate the opening of a public park in the late nineteenth century, but this area of heathland – ageless and eternal – was once a wide, open space at the very heart of the county, and it is steeped in centuries of Kent's history. As Edward Hasted tells us: 'this heath has been time out of mind used for all county meetings, and for the general business of it, the county house for this purpose, a poor low shed, is situated on the north side of it, where the sheriff continues to hold his county court monthly…'[10]

Once the site of the Saxon shire moot, in Domesday, this is 'Pinnedenna', which some believed is derived from the Old English 'pinian - den', meaning a woodland clearing where punishment took place. Hard to imagine today, but generations of Kent folk would have known the darker nature of this spot; fearing its environs, especially after nightfall, they would have skirted swiftly around the edges of Gallows Wood, and tried not to look up as they hurried beneath the swinging shadows on Gallows Hill.

Justice Peter Warburton was not a man to take fright easily; he had weathered the tempest that had swept away the English king and held onto his situation with grim determination. It was a position he had worked hard to achieve, and he had spent years cultivating a respectable reputation in legal circles. Practical, down-to-earth, and highly esteemed, in the hot summer of 1652, he was a serving Justice for the Court of Common Pleas on the Home Circuit and, that July, found himself in Maidstone. There was much excitement at his arrival, for he was to preside over a case which had attracted a great deal of local attention and fuelled the local imagination: a group of Kent folk – men and women – stood accused of the 'execrable and diabolicall crime of witchcraft'; of ruining crops, of bewitching and killing livestock, even of murder. This was to be the largest, single witchcraft trial in the county's history. Little could Warburton have predicted the wild stories he was about to hear as he took his seat for the commencement of proceedings.

Of the eighteen accused, fourteen would be convicted, and eight of them imprisoned; members of the Reynolds and Wilson families, from Grain, were incarcerated for the bewitching of nine children. It was reported that, by their

Penenden Heath today.
(© Marathon
CC-BY-SA/2.0)

witchcraft, £500 worth of cattle and seventy sheep were lost, and a ship laden with valuable corn was wrecked off the Kent coast. Thomas Creed, of Cranbrook, was accused of bewitching horses and Goodwife Jervis, from Benenden, was alleged to have killed a herd of pigs. Most sinister of all was the allegation that Alice Rayzell, of High Halstow, had caused the death of a three-year-old girl (although the jury quickly decided that this last claim was untrue). For these eight, the prospect of a jail term would have been grim, but for the remaining six of the group convicted – Anne Ashby, alias Cobler, Anne Martyn, Mary Browne, Mildred Wright, and Anne Wilson of Cranbrook, along with Mary Read of Lenham – the consequences of this trial would be far more brutal.[11]

Anne Ashby, apparently the star of the show, was called for questioning. The expectant crowd, jostling to catch a glimpse of this now infamous woman, might have been disappointed. No doubt they had imagined a grotesque or frightening figure; Ashby – perhaps in her mid-forties – was a rather ordinary-looking, unremarkable individual. But appearances can be deceptive; before long, Anne fell 'into an extasie, screeching and crying out very dolefully' whilst swelling 'into a monstrous and vast bigness'[12] in full view of the entire court. How the astonished onlookers must have gasped in horror. As Anne recovered her normal size, and the murmurings began to subside, she recounted the story of how she had been visited by a spirit called 'Rug', which, she said, 'came out of her mouth like a mouse'. The bewildered jury was also told how the same Rug had brought about the death of a groom who had been present at the time of Anne's original examination. If this bizarre display had not been enough to sway the jury's verdict against her, the accused woman then went on to boast that 'the Divell' had gifted her a piece of scorched flesh which held the power to make wishes come true. Once this grizzly article had been recovered from the place where Anne had said it was hidden, it was put on display 'at the sign of the Swan in Maidstone'[13] (one cannot help but wonder how many of those present at the court that day might later have made a stop at the Swan to try their own luck).

1600s depiction of
a witches' coven.

In English law, since 1604, the penalty for Ashby's crime of 'covenanting with the Devil' was execution, but the sentence was rarely imposed (except by the ruthless Matthew Hopkins in East Anglia in the mid-1640s) unless there was actual evidence of murder or serious damage to property. Often, the so-called 'evidence' in such cases was proffered by ill-wishing rivals or neighbours bearing grudges. However, in this case, the proof required to send these women to the gallows was provided by the accused themselves: an eye-witness's account of the court proceedings, published immediately after the trial, describes how each gave positive evidence of her dealings with the devil and his accomplices – some of them even claiming to be carrying the devil's children.

Although witchcraft was recognised as a criminal offence in seventeenth-century England, there was never any agreement upon the definition or identification of 'a witch', so an ad hoc system of assessments was used to 'uncover' a suspect's guilt. The women in this case were examined for physical defects and subjected to the accepted technique (a particular favourite of Hopkins') of 'pricking': 'A pin being thrust to the head into one of their arms, the party did not feel it, nor did it draw blood from her.'[14]

East Sutton lawyer Robert Filmer published a scathing treatise in response to this trial, just a few months after its conclusion, in which he wrote:

> in the late miserable times of Rebellion and Usurpation, the unhappy notions of the absurd power of Witches to hurt both man and beast had taken so great a possession of the minds of the credulous and weak teachers of those times, that it was thought no less than doing God service to promote the prosecution and execution of silly ignorant old women under the name of Witches.[15]

Similar scepticism had been expressed, years earlier, by another Kent notable, Reginald Scott, in his *Discoverie of Witchcraft* published in 1584. Both men took an enlightened view of the witchcraft phenomenon, urging caution, and the deployment of common sense among those called to sit in judgement over such cases: 'the publique faith of the present Age,' wrote Filmer, 'is none of the best evidence...' No such rational thought was to grace the Maidstone Assizes in July 1652.

What doubts might the jurors have had about the validity of the 'evidence' with which they were presented? Did they believe, like Robert Filmer, that the accused were nothing more dangerous than just 'silly ignorant old women'? Or were they shuddering with fear as they eyed the accused and contemplated the horrors of their dark, secret lives? These women were the poor wives and daughters of communities very like their own and a proclamation of guilt made every juryman an executioner, yet these were also self-confessed witches, and was it not written: 'Thou shalt not suffer a witch to live'? At length, the foreman rose to deliver the jury's verdict, an anxious quiet falling upon the room. Justice Warburton, whatever his own thoughts on the matter, was obliged to deliver sentence: all six women were legally convicted and 'adjudged to be hanged at the common place of execution' – that was Gallows Hill, on Penenden Heath.

Reginald Scott's *Discoverie of Witchcraft*, published in 1584 and reprinted in 1651, had set out to prove that belief in witches was 'but imaginary'.

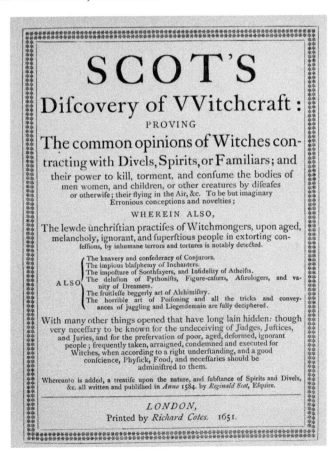

SCOT'S
Difcovery of VVitchcraft:
PROVING

The common opinions of Witches con-
tracting with Divels, Spirits, or Familiars; and
their power to kill, torment, and confume the bodies of men women, and children, or other creatures by difeafes or otherwife; their flying in the Air, &c. To be but imaginary Erronious conceptions and novelties;

WHEREIN ALSO,

The lewde unchriftian practifes of Witchmongers, upon aged, melancholy, ignorant, and fuperftious people in extorting con-feffions, by inhumane terrors and tortures is notably detected.

ALSO
The knavery and confederacy of Conjurors.
The impious blafphemy of Inchanters.
The impofture of Soothfayers, and Infidelity of Atheifts.
The delufion of Pythonifts, Figure-cafters, Aftrologers, and va-nity of Dreamers.
The fruitleffe beggerly art of Alchimiftry.
The horrible art of Poifoning and all the tricks and convey-ances of juggling and Liegerdemain are fully deciphered.

With many other things opened that have long lain hidden; though very neceffary to be known for the undeceiving of Judges, Juftices, and Juries, and for the prefervation of poor, aged, deformed, ignorant people ; frequently taken, arraigned, condemned and executed for Witches, when according to a right underftanding, and a good confcience, Phyfick, Food, and neceffaries should be adminiftred to them.

Whereunto is added, a treatife upon the nature, and fubftance of Spirits and Divels, &c. all written and publifhed in *Anno* 1584. by *Reginald Scot*, Efquire.

___

LONDON,
Printed by *Richard Cotes.* 1651.

At hearing their sentences passed, the accused – shocked, angry, frightened – made their last, desperate attempts were faced with the jeering and catcalls of the spectating mob. In an attempt to elicit some clemency, Anne Ashby and Anne Martin pleaded that they were with child. When questioned about this, they 'confessed it was not by any man, but by the Divell ... that the Divell had known them carnally, and that they and no hurt by it.'[16] A panel of matrons, called to examine the women, found their claims to be entirely false. This final revelation fuelled the fury of the onlookers and 'some there were that wished rather they be burned to ashes', for 'it was a received opinion amongst many that the body of a witch being burnt, her bloud is prevented thereby from becoming hereditary.'[17] Judge Warburton, who was not convinced by the jury's verdicts, secured reprieves for three of the women condemned, but their executions had already taken place by the time these arrived from Westminster.

This might have been the biggest witch trial in Kent, but it was not the only one. Between 1559 and 1703, there is evidence for 250 witchcraft accusations in the county and, less than ten years earlier, a case in Faversham had resulted in the execution of three – possibly four – women. Joan Walliford, Joan Cariden, Jane Hott and Elizabeth Harris all confessed to having made bargains with the Devil. Their stories were detailed and graphic, and the women were as convinced as they were convincing of their own guilt. Three executions took place on 29 September 1645; the gallows possibly stood at a crossroads near the centre of town, and would have been a sickening, but familiar, sight to locals as they went about their daily business. An execution of this scale – and for these crimes – would have been a great public spectacle and witnessed by many. The fate of Elizabeth Harris remains something of a mystery; probably, she was executed soon after, but there is no known proof of her fortune.

The Penenden Heath gallows are thought to have stood in the vicinity of the Chiltern Hundreds pub.

6
The Story of Pocahontas
(c. 1596–1617)

In the quiet garden of the church of St George in Gravesend stands an elegant statue of a Native American woman. She is dressed in simple garments and stands with her arms open in a gesture of peace, facing the slow, grey ribbon of the Thames to the north. She is Pocahontas, daughter of the great Chief Powhatan, and one of the greatest English celebrities of her day. But Gravesend was just the end of her journey; most of her brief but colourful life was played out on the other side of the Atlantic some 400 years ago ...

Confident, erudite, and well travelled, John Smith had been chosen to head the London Virginia Company's colonial venture. By April 1607, he had already soldiered and pirated his way around Europe and the Middle East, but the Jamestown settlement was his chance to find his fortune and make his mark on history. It would not be easy. Within five months, two-thirds of Smith's companions would succumb to disease or starvation and the second wave of settlers, arriving the following winter, would suffer a similar fate. Making a life in the New World was going to be an arduous endeavour, especially if the settlers had no friends. In

The statue of Pocahontas, St George's Church, Gravesend.

the early 1600s, some 10,000 square miles of what the English called 'Virginia' was controlled by the Powhatan Confederacy, an affiliation of over thirty separate Native American tribes, numbering around 20,000 people, who had long inhabited the land they called Tsenacommacah ('densely inhabited land').

Their leader, Wahunsenacawh, had tolerated the English at first – after all, these new Europeans might prove useful allies against the raiding Spanish – and Smith's own accounts, corroborated by those of Governor Percy, describe how, early on, supplies provided by their neighbours saved many of the first colonists from starvation. The new relationship was tentative, and, in the winter of that first year, whilst on an exploratory journey along the Chickahominy River, Smith was captured by Opechancanough, brother of the Powhatan Chief, and taken to Werowocomoco Village. According to Smith's recollections, he was treated as a guest, but, in a letter he wrote to Queen Anne, in 1616, he described, in dramatic terms, how his hosts' generous hospitality had abruptly changed; held on the ground, he was surrounded by men wielding wooden clubs and feared a brutal execution when, suddenly, a little girl, risking 'the beating out of her own brains', threw herself upon him, pleading with the chief, her father, for Smith's life.

This 1624 map was drawn from evidence gathered by John Smith in 1614. (normanblev-enthalmapcenter CC BY-SA 2.0, 2008)

Reconstructed Powhatan village at the Jamestown Settlement Living History Museum. (Nationalparks CC BY-SA 2.5)

Amonute (also known as Matoaka) was about ten years old, Smith supposed; a familiar sight around the Jamestown fort, she could often be seen racing the boys or cartwheeling around the marketplace Another settler, William Strachey, described the child's boundless energy and exuberance, qualities which led to her father nicknaming his daughter 'Playful One', or Pocahontas.[18] Gregarious and inquisitive, it did not take long for the child to strike up a friendship with Smith; the pair quickly began to learn each other's languages and Pocahontas prevailed upon her father to support the entire English colony through its first winter, often delivering food herself. For 'two or three years ... she next under God', wrote Smith, was 'the instrument to preserve this colony from death, famine, and utter confusion'.

Relations between the Americans and the English remained amicable, but uneasy, and Pocahontas acted a second time to save Smith, two years later, warning him of plans to ambush and capture him. As more settlers poached more land from the Powhatan Confederacy, relations between the English and their neighbours began to deteriorate and, at this point, Smith was sent back to England. He did not take his leave of Pocahontas or her father, who were informed that the Englishman had died in an accident; it would be some years before they learned the truth. The winter of 1609–10, known as 'the starving time', would prove perilous for the fragile colony, and war approached.

Historic Jamestown, Virginia. (kenlund CC BY-SA 2.0, 2003)

The shocking brutality of the First Anglo-Powhatan War would last five bitter years, and Pocahontas would be the one to broker its peace. It was, without doubt, the strength of her father's love for 'his daughter as deere as his owne life' that marked Pocahontas' value as a target for the English, who captured her in 1612. Regarding the chief as the equivalent of an English king, they supposed that Pocahontas held the status of an English princess. However, in the culture of her own people, she stood to inherit nothing of her father's power or wealth. Whilst visiting the Potowomac village of Passapatanzy, Pocahontas was betrayed and taken by Captain Samuel Argall to the second colonial settlement, Henricus, where she was held hostage under the supervision of Deputy Governor, Sir Thomas Dale, for over a year. During this time, while her father negotiated the English demands, Dale saw to it that Pocahontas learned about Christianity and she was, by his account, quickly converted. He tells us that she 'renounced publickly her country Idolatry, openly confessed her Christian faith, [and] was, as she desired, baptised', taking the Christian name Rebecca. Whether or not Pocahontas did fully convert to Christianity is uncertain; perhaps she regarded the baptism service as an initiation ceremony which suited her diplomatic endeavours, and it would not have seemed unusual to her to adopt a Christian name in the same way guests of her father were offered tribal monikers as a mark of welcome and acceptance.

There has been much debate and controversy over Pocahontas' treatment at the hands of her English captors; she left no account of her own, and we have only the testimony of her abductors by which to assess her experience. Their accounts tell us that she was well treated, respected, educated, and happy. The Mattaponi version, with a view to redressing the some of the damages of colonialism, paints a far darker picture of subjugation and even brutality. There is also uncertainty about Pocahontas' marital status at the time of her capture: William Strachey's 1614 account mentions 'Kocoum', a 'private captain' of the Potowomac, describing him, at that time, as Pocahontas' husband of two years. This idea is certainly perpetuated in the Mattaponi oral tradition of her story, but other accounts, such as that of Ralph Hamor, make no mention of her having been married.[19] There is no definitive evidence of the marriage and it would seem strange that, if she had been married at the time of her capture, the English should still have pressed her father, rather than her husband, for her ransom.

The long year of Pocahontas' captivity passed in a stalemate between her people and the English; eventually, tired of what he regarded as Wahunsenacawh's procrastination, Dale took Pocahontas and a small force to visit the chief. Pocahontas is said to have been angry with her father, and there are accounts of her having berated him for abandoning her. But she had not been quite alone during her time at Henricus: the proprietor of the Varina Farms plantation across the James River, John Rolfe, had been a regular visitor. Described by Alexander Whitakers in 1614 as an 'honest and discreet English gentleman', Rolfe was beginning to make a name and fortune for himself both in the colony and back in England, having succeeded in cultivating the sweet tobacco *Nicotiana tabacum*, which he named 'Orinoco'. Perhaps the widowed Rolfe and young Pocahontas made an unlikely couple but, in a heartfelt and poignant letter to Governor Dale, Rolfe gave his reasons for his controversial marriage, not least of which was his desire to 'indevour to make ... a Christian' of his new wife, 'whose education hath bin rude, her manners barbarous, her generation accursed'. Pocahontas and Rolfe were married on 5 April 1614, their son, Thomas, was born the January after, and the following year, the Virginia Company investors invited the family to England in the hopes that their remarkable story might inspire others to join them and serve to quiet English anxieties about the 'godless' Native Americans.

So, with about a dozen members of her wider family, Pocahontas arrived in England, there to be presented at court and entertained by the English aristocracy for the best part of a year, but perhaps the greatest surprise of her trip would be her encounter with John Smith. He appears to have avoided their meeting until the latest possible moment and, from all accounts, she admonished him for having broken oaths he had made to her father. In March 1617, it was decided that the Rolfes would return to Virginia but, by this time, both mother and son had fallen ill, and they were put off the ship at Gravesend as it made its way along the Thames. Thomas was cared for locally until a relative of his father arrived to care for him. He would return to Virginia as an adult, to claim his father's land and restore some of the peace fostered by his mother. Pocahontas, however, died just days after leaving the ship and was buried at the town church on 21 March.

John Rolfe's petition to marry Pocahontas (St George's Church, Gravesend).

The exact cause of her death is unrecorded and there are many theories about her having been deliberately poisoned, but London in the 1600s was rife with disease and it is most likely that she succumbed to a bacterial infection or one of the very common, everyday English ailments. She did not suffer for long. According to her husband, Matoaka's last thoughts and words were of their son: 'all must die,' she said, 'but it is enough that [my] child liveth'. Her burial is recorded in the parish register, where she is mistakenly referred to as the wife of Thomas, rather than John Rolfe: 'Rebecca Wrolfe, wyffe of Thomas Wrolfe gent. A virginia Lady borne was buried in ye chauncell'.

Those hoping to visit her grave today will be disappointed: the church in which Pocahontas was laid to rest was irreparably damaged by a series of fires and, in 1731, was replaced by a new edifice, dedicated to St George in honour of his namesake, King George II. Although the parish register records that her grave was within the chancel of the old church, its exact location is unknown, but a memorial tablet in the new building commemorates the 'gentle and humane ... friend of the earliest struggling English colonists'.

The statue in St George's churchyard is a replica of that created by William Ordway Partridge for the Jamestown tricentenary celebrations in 1907. It was presented by the Governor of Virginia in 1958, when the churchyard was redesigned as the Princess Pocahontas Gardens.

Above left: Stone commemorating Pocahontas.

Above right: Part of a column from the lost church in which Pocahontas was buried.

Right: Pocahontas. (National Portrait Gallery, Smithsonian Institution; transfer from the National Gallery of Art; gift of the A.W. Mellon Educational and Charitable Trust, 1942 (CCO 1.0))

Ætatis suæ 21. Aᵒ. 1616.

Matoaks als Rebecka daughter to the mighty Prince Powhatan Emperour of Attanoughkomouck als Virginia converted and baptized in the Christian faith, and Wife to the worᵗ Mᵗ Tho: Rolff.

7
The Haunting of Ightham Mote

Many have been the souls that have walked the corridors of Ightham Mote. Since the reign of Edward III, this secluded refuge has been home to wealthy and influential. Today, there is usually a National Trust guide in each of the rooms open to the public, with helpful notes to inform the wide-eyed visitors as they take in the splendour of Thomas Cawne's Great Hall and marvel at the beauty of Richard Clement's painted chapel, still proudly sporting its celebrations of the marriage of Henry VIII to Catherine of Aragon. But these walls hold another, darker, more troubling story …

In the mid-1500s, with England reeling from the shock of the Protestant Reformation, the Catholic family at Ightham, hidden deep within the Kentish forest, retained a secret priest to say their Latin masses and hear their confessions. His was a dangerous but rewarding occupation and he regarded himself a latter-day crusader, waging his own holy war against the new church of this new king. Fervent, devout, and zealous, the priest had expected to serve God with all his days, and never anticipated that his head would be turned by the charms of his mistress's young maid. The scandal that followed their liaison, together with the guilt and shame, was more than the young priest could endure and he took his own life – possibly throwing himself into the green depths of the house's moat. What became of the young woman he abandoned is less clear; some believed that, when word of the affair reached her master, he flew into a rage and ordered that the girl be walled up in one of the bedrooms. Others thought this nothing more than a grizzly legend; more likely, the girl had just moved, discreetly, to another situation. And so, the story soon passed into the mythology of the house, its characters' names forgotten.

However, during renovation works in 1872, workmen uncovered a hidden door. Supposing it to conceal, perhaps, a service staircase, they set about opening it. To their horror, what greeted them as they broke though the heavy panelling was the slim, hollow-eyed skeleton of a woman, seated, as if just waiting to be found. For years, Ightham's visitors have reported sightings of a spectral 'grey lady' and, to this day, there is a 'cold spot' in one of the bedrooms that simply will not go away – a dramatic drop in temperature that leaves you shivering, and dizzy with cold, regardless of the warmth of the sun or the house's modern heating. Whatever the reason, this much I know to be true: I have felt it.

Ightham Mote.

8
Dover Straits Earthquake, 21 May 1382

It was three o'clock and, in the Blackfriars Chapter House, the afternoon was beginning to drag. As Archbishop Courtenay rose to speak, he was aware of the sensation that he was swaying, but, as he tried to steady his stance, he stumbled forwards, grasping the air in a moment of panic. Ahead of him, parchment scrolls fell from the lectern and candles clattered to the stone floor. The gathered brethren gasped as one and, outside, he heard sounds of commotion: voices shouting and a woman's scream. Far out in the Dover Straits, an earthquake – estimated to have reached a magnitude of 6.0 on the Richter Scale – had begun rippling its way across the south-east of England. The meeting at Blackfriars, ever after known as 'the Earthquake Synod', had been convened to debate the Lollard Heresy and the teachings of John Wycliffe. Courtenay was a quick thinker; immediately seizing

(© Sandra Trois 2014 CC BY-SA 4.0)

the symbolism of this peculiar event, he declared, 'this earthquake ... portends the purging of the kingdom from heresies.'[20]

In Courtenay's see of Canterbury, damage from the quake was widespread – even the cathedral itself was threatened and lost its campanile, which was never rebuilt. Nearby, the Priory of St Augustine also suffered damage and the church at Hollingbourne, along with a substantial manor house, was completely lost. Three days after the quake hit, there was an aftershock of almost equal magnitude. A similar earthquake would occur in 1580 and, most recently, a quake of magnitude 4.3 hit Folkestone in the spring of 2007.

Hollingbourne Church – rebuilt after the 1382 earthquake.

9

The Hooden Horse

It was a clear and bitter Christmas Eve. The children, fizzing with excitement, had gone to their beds while the adults, drowsing in the warmth of the fire, gazed into its flames and swirled their glasses of brandy. All was quiet, still, and calm. Somewhere over the hill, a fox wailed its lonely call and the shriek of the barn owl echoed into the dark. As the first crystals of frost began to sparkle on hedges and rooftops, the spell was rudely broken by a loud and distinct 'clack, clack, clack'.

The party jumped up, scrambling into coats, hats, boots – as excited, now, as children themselves – and bundled towards the door. 'Bang! Bang! Bang!'; three loud knocks announced the visitors' arrival and served to waken the slumbering infants who, peering wide-eyed from quilted cocoons, careened down the stairs to join the fun. Outside, the hooders stood in the lamplight! The waggoner, whip in hand, hopped from foot to foot in his impatience to be on the move; the jockey, tumbling over and over himself in his fruitless efforts to mount up and ride away into the night; Mollie (with a thatch of beard to belie her femininity), ribbons, braids, and besom all a-flutter and there, in the centre of the group, tall, dark, and haughty in its grandeur, the hooden horse itself. No one could see (though some had their suspicions) who was the cloaked and silent figure beneath the gaudily painted horse's head, pulling the string that worked its wide jaw as it snapped persistently – 'clack, clack, clack' – in demand of its bounty. The party spilled out of the door, handing over bundles of winter apples and a few bottles of beer, a hunk of rich fruit cake and two or three precious silver coins. The children, grimly fascinated by the strange spectacle, stared in wonder, while the bolder among them stretched out curious fingers towards the horse's rope main and jangling bridle. Satisfied with the household's contribution, the happy horse made a long, low obeisance, dipping its head in gratitude, and the carolling and bellringing began.

Such was the Christmas Eve experience of many who lived across East Kent during the nineteenth century. The origins of the custom are unclear; it may be that it derives from the similar practice of 'guising', which is found elsewhere in the country and contemporary accounts suggest that, during the 1800s, the hooders were farm labourers that trudged from house to house with the aim of earning a few extra pennies for the winter months. There are varying descriptions of hooden horses' heads being fashioned from wood, gaudily decorated, and the name, 'hoodening', which has no proven derivation, is likely taken from the dark cloak or hood worn to disguise the head's operator.

The hoodeners might have resembled this modern-day group of mummers. (Photo courtesy of David Hicks) *Inset*: 'Woody', the hooden horse belonging to the Woodchurch Morris. *Inset*: 'Jason', the hooden horse belonging to the Headcorn Morris.

Newspaper reports from the local press, like this one, below, from the *Maidstone and South Eastern Gazette* for Tuesday 25 December 1849, give colourful accounts of seasonal 'hoodening':

> A party of the youthful portion of the community, having procured the head of a horse. It is affixed to a pole, about four feet in length; a string is attached to the lower jaw, a horse-cloth is tied around the extreme part of the head, beneath which one of the party is concealed, who, by repeatedly pulling and loosening the string, causes the jaw to rise and fall, and thus produces, by bringing the teeth into contact, a snapping sound as he moves along; the rest of the party following in succession, grotesquely habited, and ringing handbells. In this order they proceed from house to house, singing carols and ringing their bells, and are generally remunerated for the amusement they create by largess of money, or beer and cake.

By the mid-1800s, the practice appeared to be dwindling: a Kent journalist, writing in January 1857, says that 'Hooden horses were more common twenty years ago than now'. Between the two world wars, most hooden horses were put out to pasture, however, the later twentieth century saw a gradual revival and today the hooden horse is very much alive and can be found kicking its way around the county at Christmas, May Day, and harvest celebrations, as well as at local folk festivals.

The Woodchurch Morris with Woody.

(Photo courtesy of David Hicks)

The Moving Wood at Swanscombe

William's victory at Hastings had been hard won. Little had he anticipated the Saxons' tenacity. From the ragged edge of the south coast, the Norman cavalcade now set its sights upon London, marching towards the capital, a trail of brutalities and desolation in its wake. Every measured step fanned the flames of fear in the city, where many of the surviving Saxon nobles were gathered, and weakened the Saxons' resolve. They knew the fight was lost. The great northern earls, Morcar and Edwin, accompanied by Ealdred, Bishop of London, and Prince Edgar, the last Saxon heir to the Confessor's throne, met the Norman forces at Berkhamsted, where, with great dignity, they surrendered peaceably to the Conqueror's command.

The oldest document in the City of London Archives is a scrap of vellum, on which is inscribed the 'William Charter', granted by the newly crowned king at the beginning of 1067, in recognition of the rights of the citizens of London. It is not written in William's mother tongue, but in the language of the city itself and it reveals both the significance to Londoners of their own rights and privileges and the importance to William of the Londoners' support.

> William the king, friendly salutes William the bishop and Godfrey the portreeve and all the burgesses within London both French and English. And I declare that I grant you to be all law-worthy, as you were in the days of King Edward; And I grant that every child shall be his father's heir, after his father's days; And I will not suffer any person to do you wrong; God keep you.

In the spring of 1067, whilst the king sojourned at Westminster, word of the liberties he had granted London reached Canterbury. Archbishop Stigand and Egelsine, Abbot of St Augustine's, were among the senior governors of Kent, and they began to formulate a plan. If the people of London had been so easily able to secure the preservation of their ancient rights and customs, why should not the people of Kent make a similar demand? If petitioned with respect and in reasonable language, how could the king possibly refuse? Hearing of William's imminent departure for Normandy, the church leaders made ready to meet the king's party at Swanscombe.

Travelling from the capital, along the snaking wind of the Thames, the king's retinue passed through the greening fields and riverside villages of North Kent.

Many little woods and copses, now bursting with new leaf, gave interest and colour to the day's riding. The river, turgid and glassy from the season's rains, revealed itself now and then as the path dipped and curved. Approaching Swanscombe, the royal party spied yet another cluster of trees, with young leaves shimmering in the spring breeze – but something about this little wood was very different.

In the small hours, the men of Swanscombe had gathered among the trees. Each, armed with his sword, took up a leafy bough, a great pile of which had been cut from the deeper forest the day before. As the pale dawn broke, they huddled together, the mass of verdant tree growth disguising the true form and nature of the small, but determined, Kent force. As William neared, carrying their boughs aloft, they bore down upon him, encircling the monarch, the better to gain his attention. At the signal of their bishop-commander, the men dropped the branches and drew their steels. William had no choice but to listen as, 'with a firm countenance, but words well-tempered with modesty and respect, they demanded of him the use of their ancient liberties and laws.'[21]

The Swanscombe men asked for nothing that had not been granted London. Rather than submit to Norman authority, the Kent people drew the king into a contract; Men of Kent and Kentishmen alike would now benefit from the same special consideration afforded their city-living neighbours and the ancient rights, privileges, and traditions of their forebears were preserved.

Above and right: This monument to the treaty between the forces of Duke William and the Men of Kent stands behind the church of St Peter and St Paul in Swanscombe, having been moved in 1994 from its original location at Park Corner, where it was erected in 1958.

Stone Castle

A castle at Stone is thought to have been one of the 'adulterine' castles constructed by Stephen during the Anarchy (1135–1153). By the 1200s, having fallen into disrepair, it was largely rebuilt as a private home, accommodating the Sheriff of Kent during the reign of Edward I. Today, very little of the early construction – just the tower shown on the left side of this photograph – remains, the nineteenth-century house having been built as an addition to this historic foundation. However, there are two enduring myths associated with this hidden castle, tucked away on the outskirts of Greenhithe. The first is that the original castle was built to mark the spot upon which, in 1067, William of Normandy agreed to the peace terms of the Men of Kent, and it is certainly possible that the peace talks took place here, so close to Swanscombe. The second story is, perhaps, less credible: legend has it that this was the place at which Edward, the Black Prince, heir apparent to King Edward III, received his knighthood. The *Chandos Herald*'s contemporaneous account tells us that Edward was knighted in 1346, as the English forces arrived on the coast of France, where the young prince would truly earn his warrior's spurs at the Battle of Crécy. Certainly, Edward of Woodstock (as the Prince of Wales was more commonly known during his lifetime) and his wife, Joan, the Fair Maid of Kent, had a close affinity with the county (and a particularly strong connection with Canterbury) but this story, it seems, might just be a figment of fantasy …

Stone Castle, near Greenhithe. The square tower to the left is the oldest part of the building; the rest is a Victorian extension.

The Black Dog of Leeds Castle

For centuries, there have been tales of a phantom dog prowling the house and grounds of Leeds Castle. Some believe it to have been conjured by Eleanor, Duchess of Gloucester, who was imprisoned here, in the 1440s, after being accused of using witchcraft against her husband's nephew, King Henry VI. But the spectral shadow does not seem to be the bearer of any malice or misfortune. In the early 1900s, one the castle's residents was saved from injury, or even death, when a window bay in which she had been sitting suddenly collapsed. Luckily, she had momentarily left her seat to follow a large, mysterious, black dog which she believed she had seen disappearing through the ancient stone wall.

Leeds Castle, near Maidstone.

13
How a Kent Man Saved a Japanese Cherry

As the cool breeze drifts down from the ice-capped slopes of Mount Fuji, one might be forgiven for imagining that the pale flecks on the surface of the lake are snowflakes. But it is spring, and as the sun climbs, it illuminates a magnificent cloud-scape in pink and white: cherry blossoms, as far as the eye can see. A fleeting phenomenon, the *Sakura* blooming season sweeps northwards across Japan between February and May, lasting just a couple of weeks in each place. For centuries, the Japanese, from Emperor to labourer, have taken the time to enjoy the spring custom of *hanami* (flower viewing), holding picnics, and parties beneath the laden boughs. By day, the blossoms glisten in the gentle spring sun; by night, they glow in the warm light of paper lanterns, and throughout this brief season, the cherries are admired, honoured, and revered. The earliest literary references to the custom describe only wild and weeping cherry varieties, but, during the eighteenth century, thousands of trees were planted across Japan to ensure that everyone could enjoy them; by the 1800s, more than 200 varieties

Sakura on Mount Fuji. (© Skyseeker CC BY 2.0, 2010)

were recorded. However, some of the older varieties were lost along the way and it was down to the dedication of one unassuming Kent man that the blossoms of the Great White Cherry – by the start of the twentieth century, known only from folk tales – were returned to Japan.

Collingwood Ingram (1880–1981) was born into a prestigious family; his maternal grandfather and uncles were members of the Australian parliament and his father's family had founded, and still managed, the *Illustrated London News*. The young Collingwood developed a keen interest in natural history and became an expert ornithologist, creating a catalogue of Australian bird species for the Natural History Museum in the early 1900s. A similar project took him to Japan for the first time in 1902 and he would return with his new wife for their honeymoon five years later. Having served in the Kent Cyclist Battalion during the First World War, Ingram settled at The Grange in Benenden in 1919 where he soon developed a passion for gardening.

At this time, the now-familiar ornamental variety of cherry was fairly uncommon in Britain; here, people were used to fruiting cherry trees, especially in Kent, where they were something of a local speciality. Inspired by the two large flowering cherries he had inherited at The Grange, Ingram began to research ornamental Japanese varieties. Quickly becoming an authority in this field, he earned the nickname 'Cherry' Ingram and soon set out on a series of international plant-hunting trips across Asia. In 1926, he returned to Japan, where he scoured the countryside for wild specimens of the cherries he so loved, convinced of the danger that some of the ancient varieties could be lost if an earnest conservation project was not undertaken. During his stay, Ingram addressed the Japanese Cherry

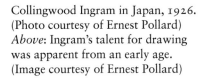
Young Skylark.

Collingwood Ingram in Japan, 1926.
(Photo courtesy of Ernest Pollard)
Above: Ingram's talent for drawing was apparent from an early age.
(Image courtesy of Ernest Pollard)

Above left: Cherry blossom in Koganie Avenue. (Photo courtesy of Ernest Pollard)

Above right: Cherries at Nikko. (Photo courtesy of Ernest Pollard)

Society and was shown a painting featuring a beautiful white cherry, known as Akatsuki (meaning 'dawn' or 'daybreak'). It was a variety which had been extinct in Japan for over a century, and yet, to Ingram, this tree was very familiar: a single flowering, large white variety with copper-coloured spring leaves and a gloriously rich autumnal show. Ingram had discovered a specimen in a cottage garden at Winchelsea just a few years earlier. More importantly, he had taken cuttings, which he had growing at home. Ingram had named the variety Tai Haku (meaning 'great white' cherry) and was confident that his trees were of the same variety as that in the painting. Collingwood recorded the coincidence in his journal: 'Mr Funatsu said he had long been searching in vain for this Akatsuki variety! It is a curious thing that it should be found again in a remote Sussex garden.'

Determined to send scions of his Tai Haku to his friends in Japan, Ingram returned to Kent, faced with the task of finding the best means by which the fragile tree saplings might be transported across the globe – no mean feat in the 1920s. At first, the saplings succumbed to heat and humidity as they were sailed across the Equator, but Ingram persevered and in 1932 – on his fifth attempt – devised a scheme of 'planting' his cuttings in potatoes, which provided sustenance enough for the journey, and sent them off northwards, overland, on the Trans-Siberian Railway. This was to be just the beginning of Ingram's conservation work.

In his Benenden garden, Collingwood raised numerous cherry hybrids, many of which he sent to Japan. He also 'adopted' over fifty endangered cherry varieties, nurturing specimen trees in his own gardens and creating one of the world's

Ingram's depiction of the cherry he named 'Tai Haku' (meaning 'great white'), later discovered to be 'Akatsuki', believed extinct for over a century. (Image courtesy of Professor Tessa Pollard)

Ingram's 'sylvan glades' at The Grange in the 1950s. (Photo courtesy of Ernest Pollard) *Inset*: Ingram was also an expert on Gladioli. (Image courtesy of Ernest Pollard).

most comprehensive cherry collections. However, Ingram was far more than just a collector: he mastered grafting methods, and pioneered new techniques to enable him to cultivate and sustain the treasured specimens with which he was entrusted. He also became an authority on gladioli – travelling the world in pursuit of their corms – and rhododendrons, many of which he grew at The Grange. In 1948, he published *Ornamental Cherries* and continued to write and publish on natural history throughout his life. Tens of thousands of trees have been propagated from Ingram's first cuttings and a spectacular tree, once thought lost, grows abundantly again across all the islands of Japan.

Written by Masuhiko Kayama and sent to Collingwood Ingram in 1932:

Oh cherries, cherries, my dear cherries
Go across two oceans and a continent safely.
You don't know England yet
But there are your friends and your kind master.
Bloom! Bloom, beautifully as in your native home
Every spring,
Your blossoms are a chain of friendship
Between England and Japan.
You are a speechless diplomat
Oh sakura, sakura, my dear Sakura.

Collingwood's gardens are still cared for lovingly. (Photo courtesy of The Grange, Benenden)

14

Dame Dorothy Selby and the Gunpowder Plot

In the chancel of the picturesque country church of St Peter in Ightham, there is a grand and elegant memorial to Dame Dorothy Selby (1572–1641), widow of Sir William Selby, of nearby Ightham Mote. Her portrait was worked by the king's own master mason, Edward Marshall (1598–1675), and the rather curious epitaph tells us that Dorothy was a dedicated needlewoman,

> Whose Arte disclosd that Plot which, had it taken,
> Rome had tryumph'd and Britans' walls had shaken...

Her 'arte' was embroidery and images from two of her works appear in the richly illustrated panel behind the bust: a representation of the Garden of Eden and a complex image of the Spanish Armada, conveying the papal conclave and Guy Fawkes to the Houses of Parliament. It is this image to which the phrase above refers; tradition has it that Dame Dorothy 'disclosed' the Gunpowder Plot in 1605, either by writing the infamous 'Monteagle Letter', counselling her cousin, William Parker, against attending the opening of Parliament on 5 November, or by deciphering the message that the letter contained. No one has ever yet identified Monteagle's mysterious correspondent, and there are many that believe the letter to have been planted by Robert Cecil. A further legend attached to this tale is that Fawke Common, in Sevenoaks, was part of the land awarded to the faithful steward to whom Dame Dorothy entrusted the delivery of her warning.

The complex memorial to Dame Dorothy Selby at St Peter's Church, Ightham. (© J. Hannan-Briggs CC BY-SA 2.0)

The Holy Maid of Kent

Elizabeth Barton was born into a dangerous age. A religious revolution was stirring, and thousands would succumb to noose, axe or flame as the Old Church fought for survival. In Aldington, a quiet hamlet in the east of Kent, the early years of the sixteenth century brought two remarkable things: the esteemed Dutch theologian, Erasmus, was appointed Rector of the parish (he would resign from the post within a year) and the Barton family welcomed a daughter that would overcome the common adversities of infancy and live beyond her tenth birthday. Astonishingly, the child would become every bit as famous as the rector. By the age of nineteen, Elizabeth had secured steady employment in the respectable household of Thomas Cobb. For a young woman of her station, marriage and a family were her most likely prospects; a life of hard work and precious little material reward – like that of her mother and grandmother before her – would have been Elizabeth's expectation. Little could she have imagined the path that fate was mapping for her when she fell ill in the spring of 1525.

For months, Elizabeth was unwell and confined to her bed; a swollen throat stole her voice, and frequent convulsions left Elizabeth writhing in agony but, whatever sufferings Elizabeth endured, there was a further, more disturbing element to these seizures. In the throes of her torment, she would succumb to a trance-like state during which, she claimed, she was visited by the Virgin Mary, who whispered divine revelations and shared prophetic visions with the dumb-struck girl. Her mind's eye, said Elizabeth, would travel outside of herself, enabling her to see the souls of the dead in heaven, purgatory, or hell. Perhaps, at first, her claims were dismissed, explained away as coincidences or the wild

Aldington is as much a quiet hamlet today as it was in the 1500s.

ramblings of a delirious mind, but when she predicted, with grim accuracy, the death of a child in the hamlet, people began to pay more heed to the strange prattling of this singular country girl.

Aldington parish priest, Richard Masters, sent word to the Archbishop of Canterbury, who despatched Edward Bocking and a party of Christ Church brethren to investigate. Bocking declared Elizabeth to be a genuine seer and so her following grew, but her affliction continued: 'shee seemed to bee in grievous paine, in so much as ... shee had suffred the pangs of death it selfe'[22] as, time and again, she spoke her warnings, in a hoarse whisper or in the deep, grumbling roar of a disembodied voice emanating from her navel. Above all, Elizabeth urged her fellow Englishmen towards greater piety, encouraging them to attend mass and confession, to take up pilgrimages, and to strengthen their faith through prayer and the recitation of the catechism. She also advised loyalty to the king and increasingly, she spoke against the rising Protestant heresy, with dire warnings against turning away from the Church of Rome.

During Lent of 1526, Elizabeth foretold a great miracle to be performed by the Holy Virgin at the Bellirica Chapel in the little hamlet of Court-at-Street. When Elizabeth set out upon her journey to the place, a jostling crowd of 2,000 to 3,000 assembled in her wake as she made her way out of Aldington, eastwards, along the Roman road. Reaching the chapel, Elizabeth prostrated herself before the statue of the Virgin and spent hours reciting 'metricall and ryming speeches.'[23] Among the witnesses were William Warham, Archbishop of Canterbury, officials from Christ Church, and members of the local gentry. Elizabeth informed her eager audience that it was the Virgin's desire that the chapel at Court-at-Street should be better maintained and endowed with its own priest, and that Elizabeth herself should enter a convent, where she might spend her days in quiet prayer and communion. Archbishop Warham, thoroughly impressed by the girl, secured her a place at the nunnery of St Sepulchre, in Canterbury.

Richard Masters was Elizabeth's parish priest at the church of St Martin, Aldington.

The remains of the Bellirica Chapel at Court-at-Street.

St Sepulchre's Nunnery, in Canterbury, became renowned – and then notorious – as the home of Elizabeth Barton.

For six years, Elizabeth, now commonly known as the 'Holy Maid of Kent', continued to communicate with the Virgin Mary, healed the sick, and worked 'wondrous myracles.'[24] Her prophesies were printed and disseminated across the country and she was fêted across Kent and London. The church attested to her honesty, her piety, and the marvel of her gift. Henry VIII's friends and first ministers, Thomas Wolsey and Thomas More, each held lengthy, private audiences with Elizabeth and, on more than one occasion, she even met with the king himself. It seemed Elizabeth's days were blessed but, as the 1520s drew to a close, murmurings of discontent were beginning to rumble, and Elizabeth might have done well to heed the whispered warnings.

By 1532, having still no legitimate male heir and becoming increasingly doubtful of his marriage ever producing one, Henry VIII had decided to put aside Katherine, his spouse of twenty years, and marry his mistress, Anne Boleyn. He did not expect any opposition to his royal will: his reasoning was practical, and in accordance with Scripture. To Henry, it was obvious that his male children had been taken by God as punishment for the king having married his brother's widow and he set about procuring a legal annulment to his 'tainted' marriage. However, not everyone saw the matter so clearly, and Henry's kingdom would be torn to pieces by the king's 'Great Matter'. Queen Katherine, horrified at being cast off, refused to acknowledge the legitimacy of Henry's actions.

Elizabeth Barton would very soon find herself standing in opposition to the might of the English crown. Perhaps she believed that she had influence enough over the king to make him change his mind – he had taken her counsel before. If so, she was woefully mistaken. In the certainty that she would be heeded, she spoke out against Henry's divorce and predicted that dire consequences would follow him into any new marriage. Henry was ever a fair-weather friend and the Holy Maid's strong voice was not one he cared to hear raised against him. Regardless of Elizabeth's grim forewarnings, Henry married Anne Boleyn and their healthy child, Elizabeth, was born in September 1533. What further evidence was required of Elizabeth Barton's deceit? The campaign to ruin her began immediately; its success would be swift.

Lurid stories about Elizabeth's private life began to circulate. Portrayed as weak, lustful, and manipulative, Elizabeth's erstwhile immaculate reputation was devastated, and her legion of followers quickly fell away. In January 1534, she was arrested along with Edward Bocking, Richard Masters, Richard Risby, Hugh Rich, John Dering and Henry Gold, as well as Bishop Fisher and Sir Thomas More – although More was later pardoned, as was the parish priest, Richard Masters. The Act of Attainder under which these arrests were made denied the prisoners any right to a trial. It was alleged that Edward Bocking had masterminded a tremendous fraud, using Elizabeth Barton as his 'diabolical instrument'[25], and steering her into asking, 'to know whether God was displeased with the Kynges Highnes for procedyng in the seid divorce.'[26] Elizabeth's response was extraordinary, and tantamount to treason. She said that, 'she had knowledge by revelacion from God, that God was highly displeased with our seid Soveraigne Lorde' and that if he remarried, 'within one moneth after suche marriage he should no lenger be Kynge of this Realme … and that he should dey a villaynes dethe.'[27]

It was alleged that Elizabeth's interference had prolonged the process of the king's divorce. Despite Queen Katherine's having rejected any communication with Elizabeth, it was said that she had been encouraged and emboldened by the nun's profound opposition to Henry. Twice, Elizabeth was called to confess to the treason of which she stood accused. At first, her supporters defended her innocence but, all too soon, she was abandoned. In an extraordinary showpiece, Elizabeth was paraded before the King's counsellors, whilst a statement outlining her crimes was read aloud. She was afforded no right of reply. This same statement was delivered in Canterbury, as well as in London, to discredit the 'Holy Maid' in the places where she had been most influential.

Convicted of high treason, Elizabeth was sentenced to death, along with Bocking, Dering, Rich, Gold, and Risby. At that time, the method of execution for female traitors was burning at the stake, as the view of a woman hanging was regarded as indecent. Elizabeth, however, was sent to the gallows at Tyburn in demonstration of the contempt with which she was regarded. On the day of her execution, 20 April 1534, the citizens of London were instructed to take the Oath of Succession, confirming the legitimacy of Henry's marriage to Anne, and of all children their marriage might produce. The bodies of the executed traitors were left to hang as a stark and gruesome warning of what would happen to any who dared gainsay the king. Elizabeth's body, along with those of Hugh Rich and Richard Risby, was eventually buried in the Greyfriars Church, Newgate, but in one final and brutal insult, Elizabeth was decapitated and as testament to the perfidy of which she had been convicted, her head displayed with those of other traitors on the stone gate of London Bridge. She is the only woman ever to have been subjected to this ignominy.

Visscher's Panorama of London (1616) shows the grizzly collection of traitors' heads on spikes atop London Bridge.

Nobody at the Door at Scotney Castle

The history of Scotney Castle (the old castle, that is, not the new house on the hill) is very much entwined with the story of the Darells, its custodians for over three centuries. Arthur Darell's 'business' was smuggling and he went to great lengths to cover all traces of his illicit trade – even, so it is believed, faking his own death and attending his own funeral service, swathed in a black cloak, where he whispered to mourners, 'that is not me'. But it is not the dastardly Darell himself that still wanders the grounds of this beautiful medieval manor.

At some point in the early 1700s, Darell, fleeing a customs officer, bolted back to Scotney, hoping that his pursuer would give up the chase, but he underestimated the man's tenacity and soon, there was a pounding upon the ancient oak door and the booming voice of the King's Law demanding admittance. Arthur knew he had no chance of escape. Flinging open the door, he took the officer by surprise and a fight ensued, in which the customs officer was killed. Gathering up the body, Darell dragged his victim towards the moat, rolled him over the edge and watched him sink until the last bubbles had broken on the water's surface. The customs man would never be seen again, but his ponderous tread and heavy hammering on the door of the old castle have been witnessed many times. Today's garden team, who often find themselves working in pairs or alone on the lawn and beds around the castle ruin, have reported hearing distinct footsteps, loud knocking and heavy thuds, but not a soul is to be seen.

The romantic ruin of Scotney Castle.

SCOTNEY OLD CASTLE, NEAR LAMBERHURST

The Goodwin Sands

'the Goodwins, I think they call the place; a very dangerous flat and fatal,
where the carcasses of many a tall ship lie buried.'

Shakespeare, *The Merchant of Venice* Act III, Scene I

Less than 6 miles out from the east Kent coast lies a platform of the same chalk
that forms Dover's White Cliffs. Usually submerged, it reveals a glimpse of its
surface at every half-tide in the form of two long, claw-shaped sandbanks. Their
name is likely derived from the Old English 'gōd wine', meaning 'good friend', a
reference to the broad, sheltered area of safe anchorage, known as The Downs,
which they provide for vessels passing through this busy shipping lane. The North

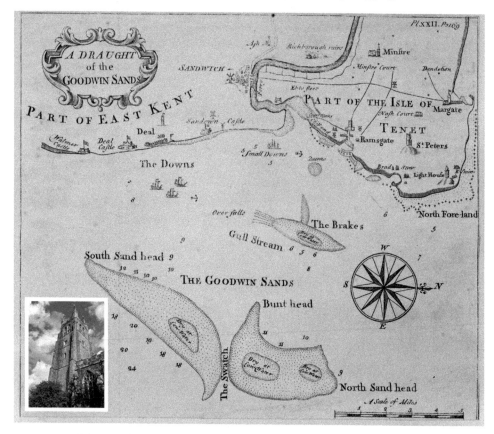

Map of the Goodwin Sands. *Inset:* The medieval tower of Tenterden's St Mildred's post-
dates the story of the submersion of the islands in 1099.

and South Callipers, as the two shoals are known, act as a natural sea defence, protecting the four-mile stretch of coastline from Deal to Kingsdown and, for centuries, locals have enjoyed the atmospheric beauty of this threshold to the North Sea. But even the best of friends can turn traitor, and only a fool would trust to the loyalty of the ever-shifting Goodwin Sands ...

Some believe that the Sands were once '*Lomea*', the island described by Julius Caesar as '*Infera insula*' – 4,000 acres, bounded by a low sea wall. In the eleventh century, the island was renamed for Godwin, the mighty Saxon Earl of Wessex who held dominion over Kent at that time. One of the most powerful men in Cnut's England, Godwin distinguished himself in the king's service and married into the first circle of Danish royalty. The dynasty he founded, though short-lived, was remarkable: Edith, his daughter, was a powerful English queen; four of his sons controlled the greatest English earldoms, and Harold, the most famous Godwinson, would be the last of this country's Saxon kings. The Godwins were charming, clever, ambitious and successful, but they were not immortal; after the Norman invasion in 1066, when the family was routed, Godwin lands were divided as so much spoil. The valuable stretch of the east Kent coast, including the Sands, with all their rich fishing ground and naturally protected anchorage, was gifted to the Abbey of St Augustine in Canterbury, but the brethren had precious little time to enjoy their gift before the island was submerged by a terrible storm in 1099, when, as the Anglo-Saxon chronicler tells us, 'at Martinmas [11 November] the incoming tide rushed up so strongly and did so much damage that no one remembered anything like it before.'[28]

The loss was seen as fitting punishment for the vainglorious abbot who, obsessed as he was by the building of a spire for his church at Tenterden, had neglected to maintain the island's coastal defences. An instance of divine intervention, a simple natural catastrophe, or did the enigmatic sands themselves seize their independence and privacy once and for all?

An alternative name for the Goodwins is 'shippe swallower'; almost 2,000 wrecks are known to lie about the shoals, and who can guess the number of souls they have claimed over the centuries? This description of the loss of HMS *Stirling Castle* on 27 November 1703 was written by J. Adams, who was on board a ship blown out of The Downs and across to the coast of Norway by the same storm:

> It was a Sight full of terrible Particulars, to see a Ship of Eighty Guns and about Six Hundred Men in that dismal Case; she had cut away all her Masts, the Men were all in the Confusions of Death and Despair; she had neither Anchor, nor Cable, nor Boat to help her; the Sea breaking over her in a terrible Manner, that sometimes she seem'd all under Water; and they knew, as well as we that saw her, that they drove by the Tempest directly for the Goodwin, where they could expect nothing but Destruction: The Cries of the Men, and the firing their Guns, One by One, every Half Minute for Help, terrified us in such a Manner, that I think we were half dead with the Horror of it.[29]

A refuge beacon in a storm on the Goodwins.

Daniel Defoe also witnessed the wreckage and records that sixty-nine of the 349 crew survived, most of whom had been able to cling to the ship's stern as the rest of the vessel was consumed by the surging currents. In the same storm, the entire crews of both HMS *Northumberland* and HMS *Restoration* were lost, and there were just three survivors from HMS *Mary*. Defoe described what he called 'the sad spectacle', visible from Deal, of those who, having survived the initial wreckage, found themselves thrown upon the exposed summits of the Sands: 'Here they had a few hours reprieve, but ... they were sure to be all wash'd into another world at the reflux of the tide.'[30]

Accounts of ships foundering on the Goodwins appear in local newspapers from the earliest editions; some are stories of miraculous near-misses or heroic recoveries, others are tales of tragedy and loss. A strange report appeared in the *Thanet Advertiser* of Friday 13 January 1950: the 'Goodwin Lights Mystery' describes how the local lifeboat crew was called to attend a vessel in distress, a short distance offshore on the night of Saturday 7th. Searching in bright moonlight for over an hour, the crew of the *Prudential* eventually returned to their Ramsgate station having found no trace of the ship. A few hours later, lights were seen again and, once more, the lifeboat maroons rallied the crew. The intrepid lifeboat circuited the sandbanks through the small hours and on, through the pale dawn, as it broke upon the inky depths of the cold North Sea. Still the crew found no ship in need of their assistance and eventually, after nearly five hours' searching, they returned to harbour, chilled, weary, and not a little bewildered.

Light Vessel 21 safeguarded the Goodwins from 1963 until its decommissioning in 2008. *Below*: This diorama of the Goodwin lightships is part of a display on board the decommissioned Light Vessel 21. *Below*: The ship's bell from the LV21. *Below*: The ship's light from the LV21.

18

The Ill-fated Voyage of the *Lady Lovibond*, 1748

Captain Reed should have known better – no sailor worth his salt would take a woman on board. But Reed was newly married and loathe to be separated from his young bride, Annetta. Besides, what did a modern man of science like him care for such antiquated, superstitious nonsense? The journey to Oporto would take his schooner, the *Lady Lovibond*, about a week – ample opportunity for Reed to impress his new wife with his sailing prowess. If there was any apprehension among the ship's company on the afternoon of Friday 13 February, no doubt their fears were somewhat offset by the prospect of a celebratory banquet in honour of the couple's nuptials and the promise of extra measures of rum that night. If his men were a little subdued as the three-mast schooner set sail along the Thames in the lowering February gloom, Reed barely noticed as he scanned his charts and cast his mind to the scything Arctic winds that lay in wait for them outside the sanctuary of the estuary. The cold night would be long and navigation of the coast challenging; better the celebration started early.

In the cheery warmth of his day cabin, Reed sat at the head of a table groaning with good food. His officers' rosy faces were illuminated by the golden flicker of candles, while, down below, the men laughed, sang, and danced and somewhere, towards the stern, a fiddle rasped a reel. High spirits and strong spirits buoyed the crew who cheered as the ship finally slipped through the broad mouth of the Thames and began to thread its way toward the Dover Strait. But not everyone was enjoying the festivities. The figure of a solitary man, hunched and swaddled against the elements, could be seen pacing the long length of the ship's main deck. John Rivers, first mate, had been best man at the captain's wedding and was well acquainted with the new Mrs Reed. Very well acquainted. In fact, he had hoped to win her hand for himself. He had found these long weeks of their engagement and the ceremony difficult to endure and, all the time, his jealousy had been simmering; Annetta's presence and this evening's revelries would prove the final straw. Rivers had helped Reed to chart the ship's course; he had read the tides; he bided his time. Gradually, the flickering lights along the coast were disappearing into darkness; the moon was high and full and lit the waves in shivering silver threads. Rivers knew that they would soon be alongside those treacherous twin banks of the Goodwin Sands. It was time to make his move.

Those who know the Goodwins are not fooled by their seeming serenity at low tide.

Stealthily approaching the helmsman, with one lightning blow, he knocked him out cold and, grabbing the wheel, Rivers heaved the ship round. Veering away from the safe passage plotted for her not hours before, *the Lady Lovibond* was now heading straight into the deadly Goodwin waters, where the fate of every soul aboard would be decided by the swirling pull of the sands and the thundering crash of the waves. Rivers would have his murderous revenge. In a matter of minutes, all but the topmost tatters of her sails was submerged. None survived.

*   *   *   *

James Westlake, captain of the *Edenbridge*, kept watch as his ship pushed around the outskirts of Deal Harbour. He knew these treacherous waters well and he wasn't about to be caught unawares. He strained his eyes against the salty miasma, but it wasn't the sight of the ship that caught his attention. Out of the leaden, February sky came the unmistakeable, bright sounds of music. There was no sign of any other vessel until, suddenly, the outline of a three-mast schooner began to manifest ahead of him, bearing down and surely certain to collide. The crew of a fishing smack watched as Westlake navigated a near-miss, but the reckless schooner passed on into the Goodwins – apparently oblivious to the dangers – where it soon began to founder and was quickly lost to the insatiable waves. A rescue mission was sent out, but no trace of the schooner could be found. Westlake recorded the incident in the *Edenbridge's* log, carefully noting the date – 13 February 1798, the fiftieth anniversary of the loss of the *Lady Lovibond*.

Fifty years later still, in 1848, sightings of a three-mast schooner – by then an uncommon ship – were reported off Walmer and Deal. Locals quickly realised that the ship was in trouble and watched with grim resignation the all-too-familiar spectacle of a ship breaking up over the broad stretch of the Goodwins. In subdued mood, they returned to their homes to prepare what they could to care for and comfort the survivors. But the lifeboat crew brought none in; in fact, they found no evidence of a ship having been there at all. The last reported sighting of Reed's phantom ship was filed in 1948, when Captain Bull Prestwick reported seeing what he believed to be a real, but strangely antique, three-masted vessel just off the east Kent coast. As it drew nearer his own ship, jolly sounds of music and merrymaking drifted across on the briny breeze and Prestwick noticed an eerie, green glow surrounding the ship as it ploughed through the waves, directly towards those sharp, twin claws of the Goodwin Sands.

There have been lighthouses at South Foreland since the 1600s and this one, built in 1843 and the first to be equipped with electric lights, served as a beacon for mariners negotiating the treacherous Goodwins until 1988. (© Chris Whippet CC-BY-SA/2.0)

19

The Staplehurst Rail Crash, 9 June 1865

When Charles Dickens woke in the early hours, he contemplated the long day's travel that lay ahead. If he had any misgivings about his Parisian sojourn reaching its end, he was, no doubt, comforted by the thought that, tonight, he would be eating supper at his beloved Gad's Hill. Others might have been daunted by the thought of his nine-hour homeward journey, but Dickens was a seasoned traveller, a globetrotter of his day, and what was a simple Channel crossing and pleasant train ride through the rolling Kent countryside to a man who had traversed the Atlantic?

Across the Channel, in the Wealden village of Headcorn, the Benge family started their day early, Henry trying his best to help his young wife, Martha, with their two young children; she might have appreciated his assistance, with their new baby due so soon. Checking his timetable one last time, Henry left for the railway, where he was employed as foreman of an eight-man platelayer gang working on track repairs. This was a recent appointment and was a position of heavy responsibility for Benge, who was no more experienced or qualified than any other man on the team.

Charles Dickens.

In the 1861 census, the twenty-three-year-old Henry Benge is recorded as lodging in a house close to the church in Headcorn.

The tidal train to London met the steamer from Boulogne at Folkestone, and Dickens boarded with his travelling companions, the young actress Ellen Ternan and her mother, Frances. Dickens and Ellen, twenty-seven years his junior, had met a decade earlier and their close relationship, about which Dickens was fiercely protective, had brought his unhappy marriage to its end. Throughout their years together, although Charles referred to Nelly as his 'magic circle of one', he did his utmost to hide her existence from his adoring public. Perhaps he tipped the brim of his top hat a little lower in the hope that no one recognised him as he stepped up into the first-class carriage. The train set off at 2.36 p.m.

Having spent weeks repairing the bridges along the stretch of the railway between Headcorn and Staplehurst, that afternoon, Henry Benge's gang reached the Beult Viaduct. Already, the dry weather was beginning to empty the river 10 feet beneath them, and it was difficult to picture, in the June sunshine, the might of it in full flood. The workmen were tasked with replacing the rotted timbers to which the iron rails were fastened. It was a simple task, and the well-practised crew would accomplish each section of necessary repairs within an hour. Henry checked, and two London-bound trains were due that afternoon, one at 2.51 p.m. and the next at 5.20 p.m. Once the first train had passed, the men set to work, removing two lengths of the rail and a piece of the baulk beneath it. Henry sent signalman John Wiles, along the line with his red flag and explosive fog signals. Railway regulations required Wiles to signal from a distance of 1,000 yards (910 metres) from the work site and to place fog warning signals on the track at 250-yard (230-metre) intervals. Wiles measured his distance by counting the usual ten telegraph poles and waited.

George Crombie pulled locomotive No. 199 and its fourteen carriages through Headcorn station at 3.10 p.m., charging over the 'galloping ground', as the straight stretch of line was known, at around 50 miles per hour, into the dazzling glare of the June sun. The journey was easy and familiar and the sight of Wiles' red flag just 500 yards (460 metres) from Benge's work site was completely unexpected. Whistling to his brake van guards and throwing his engine into reverse, Crombie did his utmost to bring the train to a halt in the short space available, but later said that he would have wanted 'at least three quarters of a mile to stop.'[31] Slowed to a speed of 20 miles per hour, the train's engine, guard's van and first carriage leapt the gap in the rails; the final two coaches remained on the far side; and the third carriage was suspended mid-air, hanging by its couplings. The remainder of the train was hurtled into the river valley below. The *Sussex Advertiser* of 17 June described the scene:

> The carriages that went down into the water were so twisted, flattened and turned upon their sides that it was impossible to say whether the unfortunate travellers inside had been killed outright by the shock, or suffocated as they lay in the water and mud...all across the ditch...lay the five or six carriages which formed the centre of the train. Through their broken sides and shattered windows were to be seen protruding human legs, and arms, and heads, and from every one of them was to be heard the piercing cry of human suffering.[32]

Dickens was in the precariously balanced third carriage, and immediately struggled to remove Ellen and Frances to safety. Then, using his hat as a water basin, he spent hours tending to the injured and dying that lay strewn all around.

Dickens described the horror of the catastrophe.

More than one of them died in his arms. Dickens described the horror and devastation in a letter to his old friend, Thomas Mitton: 'No imagination can conceive the ruin of the carriages, or the extraordinary weights under which the people were lying, or the complications into which they were twisted up among iron and wood, and mud and water.'[33] He later travelled to London and then to Gads Hill the following day. In a letter to his doctor, Francis Beard, Dickens described the accident as 'terrible' but reassured his friend that he 'was not touched – scarcely shaken.'[34] He had had the presence of mind to return to his train compartment again to retrieve the manuscript on which he had been working: the latest instalment of *Our Mutual Friend*. But perhaps he underplayed the effect the experience had upon him; for the two weeks following the crash, Dickens was unable to speak, and the memory of the trauma robbed him of the confidence with which he had previously enjoyed train travel.

Seven women and three men lost their lives in the accident, whilst over forty were injured. An inquest was held the day after the crash and, in his statement, Henry Benge told the panel he had mistaken the time of the Friday tidal train for the one on Saturday. John Wiles said that he had mistaken the passenger train for a ballast train (which would have stopped more quickly). The inquest returned that the victims had been 'feloniously killed by Joseph Gallimore [the district inspector of the section of the line] and Henry Benge', but the conduct of the train's driver and guards, as well as the actions of John Wiles, were all called into question. At the Maidstone Assizes on 24 July, whilst Gallimore was acquitted (with twenty gangs under his supervision, the inspector could hardly have been

Dickens spent hours tending to the injured.

expected to have been present at every work site at once), Henry Benge was convicted of manslaughter and sentenced to nine months' imprisonment. In fact, his sentence was reduced to six months, on account of his excellent character and exemplary service history.

The Staplehurst rail disaster would have long-term consequences for everyone involved, not least, Henry Benge, who never returned to his promising career on the railway and, instead, spent the remainder of his life working as a labourer on the farms surrounding the villages of Headcorn and neighbouring Sutton Valence. He ended his days in 1906, at Oakwood Hospital, the Kent County Lunatic Asylum, in Maidstone. Charles Dickens would never fully recover from the shock of the crash; his famously eerie story, *The Signalman,* was directly inspired by what he had experienced that June day and his son wrote that Dickens was haunted by the incident for the rest of his life. Dickens was fifty-three years old in 1865 and his health was already beginning to deteriorate. He would suffer bouts of dizziness and paralysis and a number of strokes before he died in 9 June 1870, the fifth anniversary of the Staplehurst railway disaster.

Dickens' haven – Gads Hill Place, in Higham.

20

Rochester's Role in the Abdication of James II

Sir Richard Head was an old man; through seventy-nine winters, he had steered his career and his family to make the most of every opportunity. His reputation was trusted, his many children were well married, and his prosperous estates in and around the cathedral town of Rochester were in good order. His own seat at the Hermitage, in Higham, was an impressive house, commanding a fine prosect over his beloved Kent, encompassing both the Medway and the Thames and stretching out, across the estuary, into Essex. For over a decade, he had held his seat in the Parliament – first of the Second Charles, and now of that king's younger brother, James. He had watched the new king's coronation in the spring of '85 and celebrated with his countrymen as the crown passed from one divinely appointed monarch to the next. He had listened to the whisperings of those around him as they began to fear the emergence of a new, Catholic monarchy and noticed how much more agitated those whisperings had become this summer, since the birth of the king's first son. From his position of privilege, and with the hindsight of one who remembered well the anarchy of Cromwell, Head understood the way the wind was blowing for England's monarchy; he anticipated the next chapter in the long royal saga, and he thanked his lucky stars that his own story was nearing its conclusion.

A summer of rioting across England and Scotland served to harden the attitudes of the unconvinced and the consensus was simple: King James must go. Princess Mary and her husband, William, the Duke of Orange, stood patiently in the wings as England prepared their stage. In the days immediately following the birth of the young prince, the 'Immortal Seven' – a group of disparate English nobles, united in one common purpose – had sent a letter to William, assuring him of support and success and beseeching him to save England from the menace of Rome. He arrived in November and, within weeks, the Glorious Revolution had succeeded as promised, leaving James a king usurped, heading for a life of exile. William suggested that James remove himself from the capital to Ham House, in Surrey. Instead, James travelled down the Thames to Rochester, from where he would escape to France.

Sir Richard owned several Rochester properties, including a very fine, large town house in the middle of the High Street. Entertaining high company came easily to him: he moved in exalted circles and his capable wife, Ann, was little daunted by the prospect. She was a most competent household manager and had

'Abdication
House' in
Rochester High
Street.

prepared a good table for the pending Christmas Eve meal. There was a side
of venison, good hams, and flitches of bacon hanging in the scullery; sweet and
savoury pies were neatly stored in the larder and the buttery was stacked with kegs
of Port wine, strong ale, and some of the local Kentish beer. Carefully wrapped
in muslin and tucked away for the Twelfth Night revels was the marvellous
marchpane – a beautiful angel with gilded wings. Nothing was lacking. Ann had
made sure that her best linens were aired and pressed, crisp and white as altar
cloths, the perfume of lavender still lingering, and had ordered dozens of sweet
beeswax candles to illuminate the sumptuously spread boards, where the silver
plate and Ann's prized glassware glittered in the golden glow.

Entertaining royalty – especially at Christmastide – would, ordinarily, have
been counted an honour, but in the winter of 1688 even mere association with
the now deposed King James had become a dangerous business. So it was at great
risk to himself and his family that Head opened his Rochester house to the king's
party and his genial hospitality in the dark days of that fateful December was
regarded as a demonstration of tremendous bravery and personal loyalty; James,
wishing to express his appreciation of this, presented Sir Richard with a large and
valuable emerald ring 'in token of the gratitude he felt that a subject should dare
to receive a monarch in his misfortunes, whom in turbulent times it was almost
death to call so'.

As James bade the Heads farewell in the early hours of 23 December, little did
he know that this would be the last he saw of England. Travelling directly to the
court of his cousin and ally, Louis XIV, at St Germain, James arrived in France on
25 December. He would make one endeavour to recapture his English crown, but
his campaign, driven from Ireland, was without success and he fled, to live out
his days on the other side of the Channel. Although he never attempted to return

to England after this, perhaps he still held out some hope that his crown would, one day, be restored and perhaps with this in mind, he refused the crown of Poland when it was offered him, lest that should debar him from taking back the realm to which he had been born. In his final years, James became increasingly penitent and studious, writing a treatise on government for the guidance of his son and other Catholic monarchs. After his death in 1701, there were calls for his canonisation, and parts of his body were distributed among Catholic religious houses across France.

Abdication House, as it is now called, still stands proudly in Rochester High Street, a panel affixed to the wall giving the brief details of the part this property played in the turbulent fortunes of England's royal struggles with religion. Little does this simple plaque reveal of the deep happiness James enjoyed here, or of the strength of feeling that prompted the Heads to accommodate England's last Stuart king.

Le Chateau de Saint Germain en Laye. (© Julien Chatelain, 2018)

A plaque commemorating James II's stay at what is now known as Abdication House.

21

The Battle of Goudhurst and the Demise of the Hawkhurst Gang, 1747

When Daniel Defoe visited Faversham in 1724, he noted that the town was known for its 'most notorious smuggling trade.'[35] In fact, smuggling was rife along the entire Kent coast throughout the eighteenth century. Newspapers of the period are littered with reports about smuggling runs, and military regiments were frequently deployed as the government tried – and failed – to control the serious business of contraband. Vast quantities of goods from France and Holland were ferried in through the county's busy ports; the Romney Marsh – as captured by Kent author Russell Thorndike, in his Dr Syn novels – was renowned as a smugglers' haunt, and numerous smuggler gangs fought vicious turf wars in a bid for control.

Taxes imposed on foreign goods took prices out of the reach of many 'poor, honest men' living on the wages of agricultural labour, and the attraction of cheaper, smuggled goods would have been hard for most to resist. As Kipling reminds us in his *Smuggler's Song*, 'Them that ask no questions isn't told a lie'; sometimes, it was easier to turn a blind eye to the nefarious goings on of one's neighbours.

We tend to think of eighteenth-century smugglers trading in tobacco and expensive spirits but the most valuable and sought-after commodity of the time was tea. 'Legal tea' imported by the East India Company and on which the king's tariff had been paid, was extortionately expensive, with one pound costing more than the average weekly earnings of an agricultural labourer. Smuggled 'Holland tea', on the other hand, could sell at ten times its purchase price and still be within the means of most people; little wonder it was so popular. In 1745, a proposal was put forward to reduce the price of tea to five shillings per pound in a bid to combat illegal trade. Even so, a cutter taken off the Kent coast in April 1747 had 'sixteen thousand weight of tea onboard'[36] – the smugglers knew they were onto a good thing.

In the 1700s, the Hawkhurst Gang was well known around the Kent and Sussex villages. Its members would have been familiar faces at the Oak and Ivy Inn and the Mermaid in Rye and at the Star and Eagle in Goudhurst, where they often gathered to meet. Described as 'a vicious gang of thugs who came to terrorise the population,'[37] these men were notorious for the brutality of their crimes – stories of intimidation, kidnap, torture, and murder followed in their wake. A pall of fear hung about them and, whilst children might have play-acted out half-heard, exciting tales of wild horsemanship and derring-do, their fathers were careful to keep their heads down and lock their doors as the sun began to set. Many a moonless night would have found the residents of Kent's quiet, villages and hamlets turning their faces to the wall and pulling the bedclothes around their ears to muffle the sounds of 'five and twenty ponies, Trotting through the dark.'[38] And they gradually became accustomed to a life governed by threat, menace, and violent reprisal.

Leading gang members Thomas Kingsmill and his older brother, George, were Goudhurst boys, born in the village and baptised at the church of St Mary in 1720–1 and 1712, respectively. The Kingsmills were a large and rambling family, and well-known in the small village where they made up a significant portion of the hundred or so inhabitants. Doubtless, the young Kingsmill boys ran riot in the woods and fields, and they might well have played alongside William Sturt, who had also been born there in the summer of 1718. William had chosen an adventurer's path and took the king's shilling to travel the world in his youth but, in his late twenties, returned home to settle down. Little did he know just how wild those Kingsmill boys had run.

Goudhurst's quaint village High Street has witnessed a violent history.

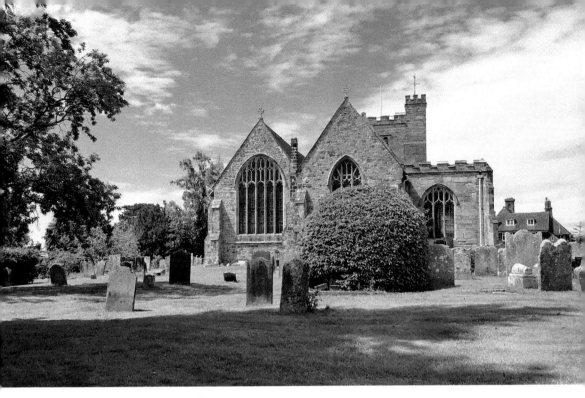

St Mary's Church, Goudhurst.

In January 1740, under the leadership of the Grey brothers, twenty to thirty members of the Hawkhurst Gang (including the Kingsmills) carried out a deadly heist in East Sussex. Newspaper reports of the shocking incident tell us that the gang, bare chested and well-fuelled with brandy, rode to Hurst Green where, 'armed with Blunderbusses and other offensive Weapons,'[39] they opened fire on customs man Thomas Carswell (who had discovered their stashed hoard of almost a ton of tea), his assistant and four dragoons. Carswell was killed at the scene and two of his officers were seriously injured. A reward of £50 was offered for the capture of any of the offenders and a rebellion against the gang began to take shape.

William Sturt made a bold move, gathering together a band of 'the townsmen of Goodhurst [sic.] ... who found it necessary to arm themselves against these desperadoes.'[40] A similar plan was unfolding in nearby Cranbrook, as the men of that town – equally in thrall to the Hawkhurst mob – also took matters into their own hands. Hearing of Sturt's challenge to his authority, Thomas Kingsmill issued a grim warning: if Goudhurst dared defy him, he would burn the village to the ground. Assembling men and arms and fortifying some of the buildings on the High Street, such as Goudhurst House and Church House, Sturt's militia kept watch for attack from the tower of St Mary's Church. The Hawkhurst Gang was known to have had tens, if not hundreds, of members, so we can but imagine the trepidation with which Sturt's men would have held their breath, but it seems that Kingsmill brought fewer than twenty men and Sturt's force was of equal number.

Left: Goudhurst House was fortified against the gang.

Below: Church House was also occupied by Sturt's men.

Newspaper reports described how George Kingsmill rode up to the Star and Crown Inn (now the Star and Eagle) and reared his horse at the door, but was shot from an upper floor window:

> Yesterday about Five o'clock in the Afternoon, 15 Smugglers went to Goudhurst, all armed with Pistols, &c. and swore they would fire the Town. The people hearing of it, got all armed and receiv'd their first Fire, but none were hurt; they fired at the Smugglers, and shot two through the Head, whereupon the others made off. The two Men killed are George Kingsman [sic], an Outlaw, who shot a Man at Hurst Green some Time ago; the other's Name is Barnitt Wollitt, an Outlaw also. They rob and plunder every Body they meet with.[41]

Wollitt was killed whilst trying to escape over the church wall. The whereabouts of the graves of these men is unknown but, in the parish burial register, an entry appears next to George's name. In Latin, it reads, *'dux scelerum glande plumbeo emisso cecidit'* ('criminal leader felled by a lead bullet').

The Star and Eagle, Goudhurst, known to the Hawkhurst Gang as the Star and Crown Inn.

Kingsmill's graves in Goudhurst churchyard is not marked.

After the Goudhurst showdown, the gang dispersed, and William Grey was picked up by the Cranbrook Association but escaped Newgate. His brother, Arthur, was taken in a separate incident of 'running, landing, and carrying away uncustomed goods'[42] and spent the next year or so awaiting his trial at the Old Bailey where, on the anniversary of the Battle of Goudhurst, he was sentenced to hang, in 1748. The Greys had been legendary and were purported to be millionaires by today's standards. Fellow gang member William Rowland was hanged with Arthur, and Thomas Fuller had been executed the year before. Now they needed a new leader and so it would be that Thomas Kingsmill, 'so distinguished for his courageous – or rather ferocious – disposition ... was chosen captain of the gang.'[43] He would not be in the post for long; Hawkhurst gangsters had bright but short careers.

The following October, now operating along the Dorset coast, Thomas led a successful raid on the Customs House in Poole, recapturing 1.5 tons of tea smuggled in from the Channel Islands on the Three Brothers in September. The mission was hugely successful until the gang was betrayed by a shoemaker named Daniel Chater. The unfortunate Chater was intercepted en route to giving evidence against the gang. They captured and tortured him for days before finally throwing him into a well. Chater's travelling companion and fellow witness, William Galley, was also taken, brutally beaten and buried alive. This heinous set of crimes was to prove the final straw for the Kent public: details of the gang members' names were printed in the *London Gazette* and they were ordered to turn themselves in. Kingsmill and around seventy-five other members were arrested and brought to trial. He was sentenced to death and hanged at Tyburn on 26 April 1749. His body was brought back to Goudhurst to be gibbeted outside his family home, a grim and dire warning to any who might seek to lift the smuggler's crown.

22

South Door at All Saints Church, Staplehurst

The church of All Saints at Staplehurst is locally known as the 'church on the hill'. It sits at the southern end of the village, peering over the busy High Street that tumbles its way down towards Cranbrook. Like many churches in the area, much of its architecture can be dated to the fourteenth and fifteenth centuries, but some believe that this place of worship evolved long before the village (which has not been identified in the written record before the 1200s) to serve a number of local manors such as Spilsill, Lovehurst, Bly Court, and Henhurst. There is some distinctly Anglo-Saxon or early Norman style herringbone pattern brickwork in the church's north wall, which might be taken as testament to its age. An early font (once found in a nearby field, doubling up as a livestock feeding trough!) and other stone carvings might further support the suggestion of its pre-Conquest incarnation, but neither the extant fabric nor the documentary evidence gives us a definitive date for the church's construction. The issue has been one of considerable local and academic debate, but there is one significant architectural feature about which passions run particularly high; it is, by far, the most striking and compelling element of the composition of the building and its origin poses a tantalising mystery.

The south door, constructed from seasoned oak – weathered, pockmarked and iron-hard – is elaborately decorated with fantastical creatures and florid, scrolling coils. Intricate overlays, the brightness of the metal mellowed by the years to a rich, chocolate patina, float over the dark, rugged, wooden boards: a small shoal of fish beneath a boat; snake-headed loops; perhaps a leaf and a crescent moon, and, above it all, a strange, winged creature taking flight. Is the story illustrated that of Ragnarok, the Norse myth of an all-consuming flood as described in the *Prose Edda* by Snorri Sturluson?[44]

> An axe-age, a sword-age, shields shall be cloven;
> A wind-age, a wolf-age, ere the world totters.
> The sun shall be darkened, earth sinks in the sea,—
> Glide from the heaven the glittering stars.[45]

The images might well depict Naglfar, the Ship of the Dead, constructed entirely from dead men's finger and toenails, carrying hordes of monsters into battle

The mysterious south door at All Saints Church, Staplehurst.

with the Gods; Jörmungandr, the Midgard Serpent, is shown writhing and thrashing beneath the waves as shoals of fish are thrown up from the depths to suffocate on the land; the stars and moon appear to tumble from the sky, while the demon dragon, Nithöggr, soars above the chaos and the world sinks beneath the fathomless sea. The keen-eyed will notice that, at the top of the door, there is a cross motif, which is taken by many to represent the protective force of Christianity and its promise to heal the fractures wrought by the Ragnarok turmoil. A glance at the top edge of the door reveals one more intriguing element of its puzzle: it has been recut to fit its current opening. Tim Tatton-Brown, who surveyed the church in the 1990s, suggested that the door – 'an exceptionally rare example of a Romanesque iron-covered doorway'[46] – was moved, after some artful and subtle reshaping, during the rebuilding work of the 1300s–1400s. He suggested that it had possibly been positioned, originally, in the nave and certainly, it is conceivable that such a remarkable and well-crafted piece would have been treated with respect, if not reverence, and salvaged for reuse and display in the newly improved church building.

This mythical storyboard has long been a cause of much scholarly enquiry and discussion: is the door a last, enduring remnant of a lost age, the shrill shriek of a distant heritage piercing through ten long centuries of Kent village life? Are we presented, here, with a genuine missive from the deep, dark wonder-world of Anglo-Saxon history? Well, there are some that argue this to be the case and the church's own webpage tells us that the door has been authoritatively dated to the mid-1000s. But there are other comparisons that suggest otherwise; for example, the work of the Herefordshire School of Masons at the Norman church of St Mary and St David, in Kilpeck, shows strong parallels with the images on the Staplehurst door. This work has been dated to the middle twelfth century but the influence of Anglo-Saxon and Celtic imagery is clearly manifest. Here, as at Staplehurst, we have swirling serpents and flourishing foliage, as well as complicated knotwork and intertwined animals. It may well be that the talented artists responsible for both churches were working contemporaneously and referencing the same sources. These were master craftsmen, working at the top of their trades, well educated and practised in their crafts, with good sponsorship and support for their creative endeavours. This was a period in which England enjoyed perhaps unprecedented cultural and artistic prosperity, and a remarkable freedom of expression can be traced in the work of its artisans. And yet, there is still a quiet whisper that insists this extraordinary artefact, with all its strange and fantastical mythological references, might just be a survivor of pre-Conquest Kent; that it might truly provide a link with Staplehurst's pre-Norman inhabitants; that it really is a doorway into the unwritten past.

23

The Kent Custom of Wassailing and Apple Yowling

Across much of Britain, people are familiar with the folk custom of wassailing, which has, in recent times, seen a resurgence in popularity, particularly in parts of the South West. The Beowulf poet regales us with tales of the 'wasail-hall' and the 'wassailing benches' of Heorot, and it seems very likely that, in this country, the first echoes of this Saxon drinking toast were heard in the Kent dominions of the formidable county patriarch, Hengist. Geoffrey of Monmouth's colourful description of the meeting of Hengist's daughter, Rowena, with King Vortigern in the mid-fifth century is the first written record we have of Kentish wassailing. At the feast at Thong Castle, held in honour of her arrival, Rowena raises a golden cup of wine to the British king, saying, 'Lauerd king, wacht heil!', meaning, 'Lord King, good health!' and, 'From that day to this, the tradition has endured in Britain, that the one who drinks first at a banquet says, "was hail!" to his partner and the one who takes the drink next replies, "drinc hail".'[47]

Usage and familiarity through the medieval period served to corrupt the Old Saxon term into the single word 'wassail', and by the close of the 1500s, it was being used by Shakespeare to describe the drunken, swaggering carousing of Hamlet's treacherous uncle. Throughout the early modern period, the written record is peppered with references to wassailing of crops and livestock between the winter solstice and Twelfth Night. If the word's etymology has dissolved into the past, it seems that, over the centuries, the Saxon salute became synonymous with a spiced apple cider drink which features as the 'wassail cup or bowl' in most of the descriptions of wassailing rituals and, by the Victorian period, no Christmas and New Year festivities were complete without provision of a 'wassail bowl' for one's guests.

A mention of Kent wassailing customs appears in the Fordwich mayoral accounts for 1585. We are told that, on the eve of New Year or Epiphany, 'the boyes and servants at those tymes shall ffrom henceforth go into any mans orchardes or gardyns to beate the trees and sing vayne songes or otherwyse belevyng therby that those trees the yere following wyll or shall yeld the more plenty of frute'.

Most of today's wassails are described as revivals of historic customs; modern wassailers, like generations of their forebears, take the opportunity to give thanks for the riches of the season just passed and to solicit a blessing for a bountiful harvest yet to come. At the start of the year, in New Ash Green, wassailers

The wassail cup and bowl, along with a hollarin' horn! (Photo courtesy of David Hicks)

Every year, the wassailing ritual is performed to promote a bountiful harvest for beautiful orchards like this one in Platts Heath. (©Max Armstrong)

gather at the village hall to form a torch-lit procession which trails down to their traditional community apple orchard. Here, singing and morris dancing, mulled cider and mince pies accompany the blessing of the finest tree, which might be decorated and illuminated by colourful fairy lights. The Keston Wassail (Keston was a Kentish village until 1965), founded by David Hicks in 2008, takes place in the garden of a local pub on the first Saturday after New Year. The garden's apple tree is first 'purified' with salt, then a piece of bread dipped in last year's cider is placed in its branches. This is a common feature of the wassailing rites, symbolising the tree's fruitfulness and fertility. In some cases, the tree is toasted or 'fed' with the cider of last year's crop.

Another essential element of Kentish wassailing rites is noise – free, plentiful and enthusiastically supplied. This has given rise to the uniquely Kent term 'yowling' (in Sussex, the term is given as 'howling'), with participants being encouraged to make as loud a cacophony as possible – hollering or yowling, blowing whistles, whirling football rattles, even banging pots and pans to accompany the great 'shout' at the end of the ceremonial reading or prayer. Perhaps the noise making was originally a means to warding off evil spirits – no doubt it would have frightened an ill-intentioned imp or two – but perhaps it was also just about having fun and letting off a little steam.

There might not be any written evidence of a continuous link between the ancient pagan rituals contemporary with Vortigern and Rowena and the modern wassailing traditions, but that is not to say that the link does not exist. Standing in the midst of a Kent orchard, the bare-branched apple trees silhouetted against a January dusk, as your breath clouds the air ahead of you and the chill of the earth creeps up, through your feet, it's all too easy to catch the whisper of an echo of those ancestral voices as they salute you through the centuries, 'Wacht hael!'.

The tree is toasted with cider-soaked bread. (Photo courtesy of David Hicks)

24

The Medway Megaliths

Britain can boast its fair share of ancient megaliths. Shrouded in mystery, they have fascinated us throughout history and continue to captivate the collective imagination. The most celebrated are popular tourist attractions, drawing thousands of visitors, but some of the oldest standing stones in England can be found well away from any beaten track, straddling the meandering course of the River Medway in Kent. The elongated Medway Megalith cluster – the only megalithic group in eastern England – is strewn across a distance of about 6 miles (10 km) and divided east to west by the river, into two sections. The western group comprises three long barrows – Coldrum, Addington and Chestnuts – and the eastern group contains Kit's Coty House and Little Kit's Coty, as well as Smith's Megalith, the Coffin Stone and the White Horse Stone. There was possibly a further barrow at Burham, to the north of the eastern group, where a causewayed enclosure has been identified. The Kent megaliths might not be on quite the same scale as Stonehenge, but their significance should not be underestimated.

Sunrise over the ancient Coldrum Stones. (© John-Christian Jacques)

The stone groupings all follow the same core design patterns; the structures are sited on an east–west axis and built from local Kent sarsen; each barrow had a burial chamber at its eastern end, and these were up to 10 feet (3 metres) high – far taller than most other British long barrows. Each site also has its own idiosyncrasies, which might point to changes of use or proprietorship, private familial traditions, or be evidence of the adoption of outside influences on Kent's Neolithic inhabitants.

Traces of the barrows' builders are faint and sketchy, but it is likely that, in Neolithic-era Kent, early agriculturalists existed alongside nomadic population groups and retained strong, historic, cultural and familial ties with their peers in continental Europe and Scandinavia. Excavations at Coldrum revealed two separate phases of burial activity in the tomb. These phases were separated by two centuries, but all derived from the same extended family group. The remains of the twenty-two individuals found here are among the earliest ever found in the British Isles and they give us a tantalising glimpse of the county's ancient society. The males were, on average, around 5 feet 4 inches (164 cm) tall, and the women around 3 inches (8 cm) shorter; they had larger than average heads and long, slender necks; their feet were shorter and wider than those of modern humans; and every one of them was right-handed.

The Coldrum Stones.

These standing stones were once the entrance to the Coldrum Long Barrow.

The antiquity of the stones and the mysteries surrounding their origins and purpose have given rise to numerous superstitions about enchantments and curses. George Orwell described Kit's Coty as 'a druidical altar or something of the kind' and the groups are often referred to as 'the Countless Stones' – a reference to a description of Stonehenge, by Sir Philip Sydney, in 1586. There are plenty of cautionary tales of misfortune befalling those who dare to trespass upon, or do damage to, the enigmatic dolmens; nonetheless, many attempts have been made to dismantle the chambers and level the sites. The Addington Long Barrow – which has delivered up no skeletal remains – has been in its ruined state throughout recorded history; by the nineteenth century, a road had been driven through the site and pieces of sarsen can be seen in many surrounding buildings. The Chestnuts barrow, built on land which had been in use and occupation during the Mesolithic, had already been ruined by the end of the medieval period, mainly through ploughing and agricultural activities. The remains of at least ten individuals were found here, in some 3,500 pieces of cremated bone. Cremation was very unusual in Britain at this time, which suggests that the barrow was a site of special significance and possibly linked with continental population groups. Arrow heads, a clay pendant and several decorated, clay pots, along with hundreds of sherds of Windmill Hill pottery, were uncovered here. A dig in 1957 also revealed masses of Mesolithic flint-knapping detritus and evidence of constant occupation up to the late medieval, at which point it seems the chamber was deliberately demolished (perhaps due to its un-Christian origins) and its stones purposely broken up.

Above: At Coldrum, some
stones remain at the top of the
barrow mound.

Right: Pieces of the Addington
Long Barrow are scattered across
both sides of the lane.

Kit's Coty House & Little (or Lower) Kit's Coty were, perhaps, named for their purpose; 'cot', meaning 'house' and 'kit', from the Old English 'gyte', meaning shedding, possibly indicating that these were believed to have served as charnel houses. Local mythology shrouds these stones. Generations of Medway folk are said to have believed that Kit's Coty capstone held a magical bowl of water that could never evaporate; some held the belief that the tombs were memorials to two ancient Kentish kings, killed in battle; others claim their construction to have been the work of witches who lived on Bluebell Hill – and who are we to argue otherwise? Little Kit's Coty's twenty-one jumbled stones belie the monument's former majesty, for this was possibly once one of the largest barrows of the group. It was also deliberately dismantled; at the end of the seventeenth century, one local landowner saw its large, flat building blocks as ideal road-surfacing material. Eminent eighteenth-century antiquarian William Stukely, who visited the site in the 1720s, spoke to residents who remembered the stones in situ but explained to him that the blocks had been too large for use in the road and so the scheme had come to nought.

The entrance to the Kit's Coty House Long Barrow.

This stone inside the barrow entrance has been inscribed by Victorian vandals.

Above: Kit's Coty House commands the brow of the hill. (© John-Christian Jacques)

Below: Remains of the barrow at Little Kit's Coty. (© John-Christian Jacques)

Human remains were found at the sites of all three of the smaller stone groups during the 1800s. The Coffin Stone (situated between the two 'Kits') is, in fact, a group of three, all now laying horizontally, but with a socket hole nearby suggesting that at least one was originally upright. The White Horse stones (upper and lower) had been broken up by 1834 but might have formed parts of a chamber. Although no trace of an earthen mound has been found, a longhouse-type building and a small, circular building of late Neolithic date have been traced to the south of this collection, which lies close to Smythe's Megalithic Barrow, on Warren Farm. Named for Clement Smythe, who, with Thomas Charles, supervised the exposure of the buried stones in 1822, this tomb was destroyed by its excavators immediately after it was discovered. Three large stones, buried inches beneath the topsoil, were hauled away to reveal the burial chamber pavement, along with a collection of human remains. These were scattered by the workmen but Smythe was able to salvage some fragments, which attested to there having been at least two individuals within the long-hidden cell.

Great Storm of February 1287

The west tower of New Romney's church of St Nicholas is an impressive monument to its Norman builders. One is struck by the warm glow of the Caen stone – so beloved by Duke William – and the 'dog-tooth' detailing around the entrance arch, but there is something else, something unusual: its doorway, approached via a short flight of steps, appears to be sunken beneath the road, and inside, there are curious tidemarks on the sturdy Romanesque pillars. The church, which has stood for a millennium, bears silent witness to an event in its early life that changed the face of the town around it. In February 1287, a tremendous storm deposited tons of sediment around the Kent coastline, redrawing the map, rerouting the River Rother and reconfiguring the fortunes of the county's southernmost Cinque Port towns. New Romney, once a major port, was transformed into an inland town, a mile from the coast. In the course of that winter night, the town was inundated with mud, sand and shingle carried from Dungeness, its ground level was raised by 5 inches (13 cm) and its harbour, which had been silting up, gradually, for decades, was rendered completely impassable. With the Rother diverted away from it, the town, along with neighbouring Lydd, lost its access to the sea and, with that, a vital source of trade.

St Nicholas' Church, New Romney. The road level is several feet above the floor level of the church, as can be seen here, at the side entrance. (© Masayuki (Yuki) Kawagishi CC BY 2.0)

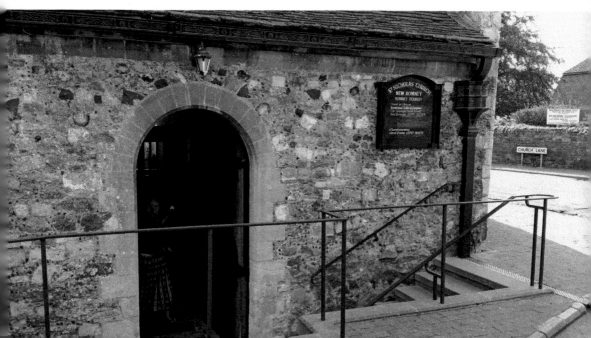

Henry V's Warship at Smallhythe

In their efforts to claim and contain the vast and variable Romney Marsh, Kent landowners have long sought to control the River Rother. In the 1300s, Geoffrey de Knelle ordered the construction of the 'Knelle Dam' to guide the river's flow around the north of the Isle of Oxney and, as a result, Smallhythe, now given access to the sea, quickly became one of the foremost shipyards in the country. It was here that 100-ton vessels were built for the navy of Henry IV, and Henry V's revolutionary 1,000-ton warship, the *Jesus*, was constructed in the early 1400s. Even into the mid-sixteenth century, large ships, such as Henry VIII's 300-ton *Great Gallyon*, were being built here. However, the shifting marsh eventually reclaimed the levels around Oxney, and Smallhythe had lost its shipyard by the start of the seventeenth century.

Even in the early twentieth century, the River Rother was still navigable up to Smallhythe.

The Isle of Oxney.

27

The Possible Origins of Some Kent Place Names

Place names reveal much about the story of an area's settlement or the ownership of land. In Kent, most placenames derive from Old English and there are several word elements that occur repeatedly, such as burgh (fortified place or stronghold), dun or ton (hill), hām (village or small settlement), hyrst (wooded hill), stān (stone), and ing, from ingas (the people, or followers, of). The word part den(n), which appears in many Wealden placenames, especially, is an old Kentish word describing a woodland clearing. These elements are most often joined to the names of individual people or prominent topographical features to give us the names with which we are familiar.

Ashford – (Old English) Æscet ford – 'clump of ash trees by a ford'
Benenden – (Old English and Old Kentish) 'the woodland pasture of Bionna'
Canterbury – (Old English) 'the burgh (stronghold) of the Cantware'
Dover – named for the stream, dobras, 'the waters'
Egerton – 'the farm of Ecgheard' (Old English)
Faversham – 'the village of the smith', from the Old English fæfer and hām
Gravesend – from the Old English graf ende, 'the end of the copse'
Herne – 'a curve or corner of land' (from the Anglian)
Ightham – 'Ehta's homestead', from the Old English Etha hām
Joyce Green – the only placename in Kent beginning with the letter 'J', Joyce
    Green was the name of the farm that covered this area near Dartford
Kemsing – 'the place of Cymesa's people' (Old English)
Leigh – from the Old English, 'a glade'
Maidstone – commonly believed to derive from Old English mægden stān,
    probably 'the stone of the maiden' – perhaps an important meeting place. The
    name might also be a corruption of the Saxon 'Medwegestun' – or Medway's
    town.
Nackington – (Old English) næting dun, 'a hill at the wet place'
Otham – 'Otta's homestead', from the Old English Otta hām
Pluckley – from the Old English leah, 'a clearing or meadow, belonging to Plucca'
Queensborough – the stronghold of the Queen (from the Old English cwen
    and burgh), this place was renamed for Philippa of Hainault (c. 1313–69),
    the queen of Edward III (1312–77), having previously been known as 'King's
    borough'

Rochester – once possibly known by the British name of Hrofi, then the Latin Durobrivis, 'a walled town with bridges'

Staplehurst – from Old English stapol hyrst, 'pillar on a hill'

Teston – from the Old English tær stān, 'the cleft stone'

Ulcombe – from the Old English ule cumb, 'the owl's cup (or valley)'

Vigo Village – the only placename in Kent beginning with the letter 'V', the hamlet was named for the Vigo Inn, which acquired its name after the Battle of Vigo Bay in 1702.

Whitstable – from Old English hwīt (white) or wita (counsellor – as in witan) and stapol (pillar or post) – likely a meeting place for a court or council, or a place known for its infertile (white) land.

Yalding – 'the place of Ealda's people' from the Old English, Ealda ingas

Notes

Hengist and Horsa

1. Giles, J. A. (translator), *The Works of Gildas and Nennius, Translated from the Latin* (London 1841) p. 15
2. Ibid, p. 16
3. Garmonsway, G. N., *The Anglo-Saxon Chronicle* (Everyman, London, 1986), p13
4. Ibid
5. Giles, J. A. .(translator), *The Works of Gildas and Nennius, Translated from the Latin* (London 1841), pp 19–20
6. Garmonsway, G. N., *The Anglo-Saxon Chronicle* (Everyman, London, 1986), p. 13
7. Bell, W. (translator), and Sprott, T., *Chronicle of Profane and Sacred History, 1851* (Forgotten Books, London, 2018), p. 30
8. The Walhalla, or Hall of High Honour, was designed by Ludwig and opened in 1842, as a reminder of German heritage in the aftermath of the Napoleonic wars. Spanning almost 2,000 years of German history, it features busts and memorial plaques honouring almost 200 of that nation's greatest heroes.

Holly Boys and Ivy Girls

9. *Gentleman's Magazine*, March 1779 https://archive.org/details/sim_gentlemans-magazine_1779-03_49_3/page/136/mode/2up [Accessed 24.10.2022]

Penenden Heath Witch Trial, 1652

10. Hasted, Edward, *The History and Topographical Survey of the County of Kent* (1778–99)
11. Elizabeth Hynes is also commemorated on the memorial at the Penenden Heath Recreation Park, but her story does not feature in the reports about this 1652 trial.
12. *An Account of the Trial, Confession and Condemnation of Six Witches*, at Maidstone, in The County of Kent, at the Assizes Held There July 1652
13. This was possibly an inn in the High Street.
14. *An Account of the Trial, Confession and Condemnation of Six Witches*, at Maidstone, in The County of Kent, at the Assizes Held There July 1652
15. Filmer, R., *An advertisement to the jurymen of England touching witches* (London, 1653)

16. *An Account of the Trial, Confession and Condemnation of Six Witches*, at Maidstone, in The County of Kent, at the Assizes Held There July 1652
17. Ibid

The Story of Pocahontas (c.1596-1617)
18. Major, Richard Henry, *The Historie of Travaile Into Virginia Britannia by William Strachey*, 1610–12, 1849
19. Hamor, Ralph, *A true discourse of the present estate of Virginia, and the success of the affaires there till the 18 of June, 1614* (Virginia State Library, 1957)

Dover Straits Earthquake, 21 May 1382
20. Wylie, J. A., *The History of Protestantism*, (Delmarva Publications, 2013), p. 198

The Moving Wood at Swanscombe
21. Hayward, John, *The Lives of the III Normans, Kings of England: William the First, William the Second, Henrie the First* (London, 1613)

The Holy Maid of Kent
22. The Project Gutenberg eBook [#38513], https://www.gutenberg.org/files/38513/38513-h/38513-h.htm#WILLIAM_I [Accessed 07.10.2022]
23. Lambarde, William, *A perambulation of Kent, conteining the description, hystorie, and customes of that shire; written in the yeere 1570, first published in the year 1576, and now increased and altered from the author's owne last copie* (London, 1826), p. 171
24. Ibid, p. 173
25. Ibid, p. 174
26. *Great Britain. The statutes of the realm: Printed by command of his majesty King George the Third, in pursuance of an address of the House of Commons of Great Britain.* From original records and authentic manuscripts, 1810–1828. (London: Dawsons of Pall Mall, 1963) Volume III, pp. 446–451.
27. Ibid

The Goodwin Sands
28. Garmonsway, G. N., *The Anglo-Saxon Chronicle* (Everyman, 1986), p. 235
29. Defoe, Daniel, *The Storm*, Project Gutenberg e-book (London, 1704) page 174.
30. Ibid, p. 135

The Staplehurst Rail Crash, 9 June 1865

31. *Reynolds's Newspaper* 25.06.1865, www.britishnewspaperarchive.co.uk [Accessed 23.07.2022]
32. *Sussex Advertiser* 17.06.1865, www.britishnewspaperarchive.co.uk [Accessed 23.07.2022]
33. Storey, G. (ed.), *The Letters of Charles Dickens Vol 11 1865–1867* (The Clarendon Press, Oxford, 1999), p. 56
34. Letter from Charles Dickens to his Doctor, 10th June 1865, Railways Archive https://www.railwaysarchive.co.uk [Accessed 22.07.2022]

The Battle of Goudhurst and the Demise of the Hawkhurst Gang, 1747

35. Defoe, Daniel, *A Tour Through the Whole Island of Great Britain 1661–1731* (Webb & Bower, Exeter, 1989), p. 41
36. *Derby Mercury* Friday 3rd April 1747 https://www.britishnewspaperarchive.co.uk/viewer/bl/0000189/17470403/011/0003 [Accessed 21.06.2022]
37. Mepham, John, *Heart of the Garden* (Apple Pie Publishing, 1992), p. 15
38. Kipling, Rudyard, *A Smuggler's Song* (1906)
39. *Stamford Mercury*, Lincolnshire, Thursday 22 January 1740 https://www.britishnewspaperarchive.co.uk/ [Accessed 21.06.2022]
40. *The Gentleman's Magazine* Volume 17, 1747 https://archive.org [Accessed 21.06.2022]
41. *Derby Mercury*, Friday 24 April 1747 https://britishnewspaperarchive.co.uk/viewer/bl/0000189/17470424/010/0003 [Accessed 24.06.2022]
42. Old Bailey Proceedings Online (www.oldbaileyonline.org, version 8.0, 24 June 2022), April 1748, trial of Arthur Gray (t17480420-23).
43. http://www.exclassics.com/newgate/ng228.htm [Accessed 23.06.2022]

South Door at All Saints Church, Staplehurst

44. Snorri Sturluson (1179–1242) was an Icelandic politician, scholar and poet.
45. *Prose Edda*, Mythopedia, 1 Sep. 2021, https://mythopedia.com/topics/prose-edda [Accessed on 20.10.2022]
46. Tatton-Brown, T., *Canterbury Diocese: Historical and Archaeological Survey*, https://www.kentarchaeology.org.uk/ [Accessed 20.10.2022]

The Kent Custom of Wassailing and Apple Yowling

47. Thorpe, Lewis (translated), *Geoffrey of Monmouth, The History of the Kings of Britain* (Penguin, 1983), p. 159.

Select Bibliography and References

Ashbee, P., 'The Medway Megaliths in a European Context' in *Archaeologia Cantiana*, 119, pp. 269–284 (1999)

Batchelor, Gordon W., *Goudhurst & Kilndown, Parish Past* (Goudhurst & Kilndown Local History Society, 1991)

Bohn, W. S., and McDevitte, W. A. (translator), *Julius Caesar's Gallic War* (1st Edition, New York: Harper & Brothers, 1869, Harper's New Classical Library)

Colyer-Fergusson, T. C., 'Pedigree of Selby Family of Ightham Mote, and Registers', *Archaeologia Cantiana* 27 (1905), pp 30–36

Filmer, R. *An Advertisement to the Jurymen of England Touching Witches* (London, 1653)

Gent, E. G and H. F., *A prodigious & tragicall history of the arraignment, tryall, confession, and condemnation of six witches at Maidstone, in Kent* (London, 1652)

Harrison, Edward, 'A Note on Dame Dorothy Selby and the Gunpowder Plot', *Archaeologia Cantiana* 42 (1930), pp 177–178

Maxwell, D., *Unknown Kent* (Bodley, 1921)

Page, William (editor),'Houses of Benedictine nuns: The priory of St Sepulchre, Canterbury', in *A History of the County of Kent: Volume 2* (London, 1926), pp 142–144. British History Online http://www.british-history.ac.uk/vch/kent/vol2/pp142-144 [accessed 21 November 2022]

Scott Robertson, Revd W. A., 'Church of All Saints, Staplehurst', *Archaeologia Cantiana* 9 (1874), pp 189–202

Service, A., *The Buildings of Britain Anglo-Saxon and Norman* (Barrie and Jenkins, 2007)

Thorpe, Lewis (translated by), *Geoffrey of Monmouth, The History of the Kings of Britain* (Penguin, 1983)

Zell. M. (editor), *Early Modern Kent 1540–1640* (Boydell Press, 2000)

https://archaeologydataservice.ac.uk/archiveDS/archiveDownload?t=arch-1132-1/dissemination/pdf/062/062_190_191.pdf

https://archive.org

https://archives.canterbury-cathedral.org/CalmView/Overview.aspx?s=staplehurst

https://britishlistedbuildings.co.uk/101060713-church-of-all-saints-staplehurst#. YvoePXbMKUk

https://www.british-history.ac.uk/survey-kent/vol7/pp119-129#highlight-first

https://www.britishnewspaperarchive.co.uk/

https://www.discoveringbritain.org/activities/south-east-england/viewpoints/ coldrum-stones-viewpoint.html [Accessed 09.06.2022].

http://www.exclassics.com/newgate/ng228.htm

http://www.goudhurstlocalhistorysociety.org/

https//www.hathitrust.org/access

https://historyofjapan.co.uk/2020/05/22/falling-blossoms/ [Accessed 31.05.2022].

https://www.oldbaileyonline.org/browse.jsp?id=t17480420-23&div= t17480420-23 – Trial of Arthur Gray 20th April 1748 https://www.railways archive.co.uk/documents/BoT_Staple1865.pdf [Accessed 31.05.2022].

https://www.railwaysarchive.co.uk/documents/Dickens_Staple1865.pdf. [Accessed 31.05.2022].

Acknowledgements

My thanks to everyone who offered me help or support in my research for this book. Especially to Max Armstrong and John-Christian Jacques (jcj@john-christianjacques.co.uk), for the use of their photographs; Ernest and Veryan Pollard; Jackie Gaynor; Bill Adie; David Hicks; Revd Jim Fletcher and the Churchwardens of St George's Church, Gravesend; Päivi Seppälä of the Light Vessel 21 (www.lv21.co.uk); and the generous souls who share their images through Creative Commons. If I have inadvertently used copyright material without permission, I apologise and will make the necessary correction at the first opportunity.

Thank you to P.K., for traipsing across the county with me, and to my mum, Jean, for being my adventuring companion.